Forex Trading for Beginners

What Everybody Ought to Know
About the Day Trading Business,
How to Understand the Forex
Market, Scalping Strategies, and the
Secret of Making Money Online

Bill Sykes / Timothy Gibbs

Table of Contents

Introduction

Imagine being part of the most liquid market in the world.

How liquid? We are talking about a market that trades in currency worth $5,100,000,000,000. That's 5 trillion dollars by the way[1].

Now, maybe that number doesn't sound all that exciting. After all, if you had to combine the number of transactions taking place around the world, then perhaps 5 trillion isn't such a large number. At some point, that number will be reached anyways.

But what if you realized that the above mentioned 5 trillion dollars is the currency traded in one day.

Yes, just a single day.

Applying basic math, we are looking at $1,861,500,000,000,000 worth of transactions taking place in a year. Which is why more and more people are jumping on the Forex bandwagon, hoping to take even an infinitesimal portion of the amount traded in a day. Think about it this way, even if you thought that perhaps you might aim for a small percentage of that amount, maybe just 0.001%. You don't want to be greedy here. Let's take it slow.

That still gives you $51,000,000.

That is still a huge amount. That is big money. And that is one of the reasons why Forex has been growing recently.

At one point, Forex was the realm of the "big shots". We are talking about global banks, multinational corporations, hedge funds, and wealthy investors. It seemed like a private club that was meant only for the elite.

But the liquidity of the market combined with the rise in internet technologies changed all that. That is why you can see tens of thousands of traders from around the world who have joined in on the challenges and excitement of trading in the Forex market. With the increase in accessibility (using trading apps for example) and the ability to get started with as little as $25, the allure of Forex is too hard to resist.

But the Forex market is not all about simply deciding to invest a bit of money, waiting for a year or two, taking out the cash, buying your own private island, building a castle, and retiring to sip mojitos and watch The Avengers reruns on a 100-inch screen.

You can't just think that by aiming for 0.001% of the currencies traded in a single day and investing a small bit of money, everything will simply happen on its own.

There is more to it than that. You need to be smart. You need to be patient. You need to be precise. And these are not just random things added here to inflate the importance and challenges of Forex. They are what you should be aiming to become.

Take for example the story of the financial analyst at a Canadian pharmacy[2]. He tried to bet big on a volatile market but ended up losing all his life savings.

But within all the stories spreading about Forex, there are numerous successes as well.

Think of the story of Bill Lipschutz. He made hundreds of millions of dollars in profits in the 1980s at an Fx department. The best part? He had no prior experience in trading with currencies. None. Zip. Nada.

Even if you have previous experience with the Forex market, it does not mean that you are ready to face the unexpected situations that crop up. After all, Forex is highly predictable. In fact, Bill Lipschutz (the trader we just mentioned in the example above) says that the key to becoming a successful trader is trying to make money when you are right probably 20 or 30 percent of the time.

Try and put that into perspective and imagine why one of the most successful traders in the world believes that you will be right a rather low percentage of the time. His statement is not an indication of the intelligence of the traders. He is not saying that you are too dumb to do anything right.

Rather, he is talking about the severe unpredictability of the Forex market. He is talking about being prepared and having the right knowledge to figure out what to do in any situation.

And that is what you have here with you.

You hold in your hands a compendium of knowledge that helps you better understand the Forex market.

You are going to learn more about the Forex market, what it is, and why it has seen an explosion of growth in recent years. You are going to understand how to get into a winning mindset and the things you should avoid in order to have a rational and logical state of mind (very important when you are trading).

We will then look at the different ways that you can tackle trading, how to begin your trading journey, and how to form a strong battle plan.

We are also going to look at some of the tools that traders use to stay ahead of the game.

We are going to make your foray into Forex a smooth process.

However, this comes with a caveat.

Remember that at the end of the day, you will be making the tough choices. There are no get-rich-quick tactics in Forex trading. It all depends on your actions. Of course, this book will help you navigate many of the complexities of the Fx market, but in the end, you will be the one taking charge of your trading.

Which is why, one of the biggest pieces of advice that you should stick to is that you should never, ever, EVER make assumptions about a trade without having all the information or knowledge about the market. In the world of Forex, more is always welcome. And by more, we are referring to more information. You see, information is the currency you use before you even begin working on the actual currency. It might not seem that obvious in the beginning. You might be trading on small amounts and the losses might look like lessons. But as you increase your trades, you are going to find out that the risk increases exponentially.

Zig Ziglar, the popular salesman and motivational speaker is quoted aptly, "The best time to do something significant is between yesterday and tomorrow."

That is why it is never too late to learn something and develop yourself.

This book will help you learn, understand, and navigate the world of Forex.

Welcome to Forex Trading for Beginners.

Chapter 1: Welcome to Forex Exchange Trading!

What is Forex?

The term "Forex" is often shortened to "FX", but the word itself is also an abbreviated version of two words "FOReign EXchange".

Forex is a global trading market that provides a platform for businesses, banks, public entities, corporations, and private investors to exchange certain currencies. This exchange allows the parties to either make commercial transactions or merely speculate on the currencies.

Now, this might remind you of another form of market, the Stock market. But the two function in entirely different ways. For one, Forex deals with currencies. Secondly, stock markets have a fixed schedule that they adhere to. On the other hand, Forex is open to the public 24 hours a day for 5 days a week.

Forex begins its activities at 5 p.m. on Sunday, Eastern Time, and then closes the market at 4 p.m. on Friday (ET). This allows people to trade from anywhere in the world, no matter what time zones they follow. This degree of market availability is possible because there are always markets that are open around the globe. Additionally, gone are the days when traders have to be physically present at a certain venue to conduct their trades. Today, you simply have to boot up your internet or your mobile app, select your trading portal, and conduct your activities.

Forex does have a few "main markets" or centers where the majority of the action takes place. These markets are located in Sydney, London, Zurich, China, New York, Toyko, and Frankfurt. But again, you do not have to be there physically to conduct your trades.

When you are performing a transaction in the Forex market, then you are doing two things simultaneously:

1. You are buying one currency.

2. You are selling another currency.

In other words, currencies are traded in pairs and if you open a Forex platform, then you might notice currencies labeled as GBP/USD (which is short for pound sterling/U.S. dollar) or USD/CAD (U.S. dollar/Canadian dollar) to cite a few examples.

When dealing with pairs, you have two components to focus on. The first is the base currency, which is the first currency in the pair. The second component is the counter currency, which is the second. Let us take one of the examples of currencies we just mentioned above.

In the GBP/USD pair, GBP is the base currency and USD is the counter currency or quote currency.

When you trade, you are typically doing it under the idea that the value of the currency you are buying increases when compared to the value of the currency you are selling. If this happens, then you typically sell the position and make a profit.

Why Trading Forex is Better Than Other Options

There are three main reasons why Forex is better than choosing other avenues for trading, be it stocks, bitcoin, or even options. We have already explored one of the options, so let us start with that.

Forex is Highly Liquid

The stock market trades in roughly $10 billion in volumes in a single day. But what is that compared for Forex? In fact, that does not even amount to 1% of the total trades carried out per day in the Fx market.

Better Information

Forget Tyco. Forget Enron. Forget all the other companies that provide you with information about companies, bitcoins, or markets. When you work with Forex, you are not dealing with the knowledge provided to you by a few entities. You are looking at the strengths and trends of an entire economy. An economy at such a scale will have multiple reports surrounding it. This means you get more accurate information about your trades.

Closing

Other markets have to close at the end of the day. Not Forex. This gives you flexibility when it comes to trading. You can choose when and how you would like to trade.

These are just some of the reasons why you should venture into Forex. We are going to look at a lot more further below.

Why Forex?

At the core of Forex, you are dealing with currency trading. And at the core of that currency trading, you have speculation about the values of currencies.

Hold on, you say.

Speculation? You ask. Didn't you tell me not to assume anything? Now you are telling me to go ahead and speculate?

Of course, you are going to speculate. But before we get to that, let us cover some of the basics first.

Currency trading is speculation. It is as simple as that. You are using what knowledge and information you have to make a profit by buying currencies. It is like buying stocks or any other financial security; you make a transaction and hope to make a profitable return on it. However, in the Forex market, the securities you are dealing with concern the currencies of nations.

But in the world of Forex, speculation is not based on blind assumptions. It is not even gambling (even though some people might think that it is so). When you gamble or make a guess, you are playing with your money even though you know that the odds are against you. You just hope that, given time, lady luck will smile at you with teeth so white that you could use them as floodlights. Typically, when you invest, you are aiming to minimize the risks and maximize the return over a certain period of time (usually months or years). In Forex, you are maximizing returns over a short period of time (usually minutes, hours, or days). This involves speculating (or also known as "active trading" in the

Forex world) where you adopt calculated financial risks in order to gain a profit.

And there you have the keyword that comes into play when describing Forex: calculated. You are not just sitting blindly twiddling your thumbs hoping to make it rich. You are going to read the trends, understand the shifts, and even use the latest news to make calculated risks.

The best way to understand your actions is by taking the example of a business. If you are the owner of a business, then you are going to be making calculated risks. Should you increase the available stock that you have? Do you want to hire more employees? Should you think about expanding your business or opening a branch in another location? Do you need to spend heavily on big marketing campaigns?

You may never be certain about the outcomes of any of those decisions. But you do make choices based on the information you have. For example, you notice that there is a demand for your products in another state. After conducting a market survey, you decide that it would be profitable for you to have a branch in that state. You immediately open up another business.

But what if you are not receiving profits that way you had expected? What are you going to do then? Are you going to pack up and call it quits? Or will you try some other tactics to attract customers to your business?

It is the same with Forex. When you speculate, you are making decisions about your investment based on the information you have with you.

This is why not many people realize before venturing into Forex that they need to be equipped with a certain frame of mind and skill set (thankfully, you have this book).

- You need to be dedicated. You can invest in the Forex market and ignore it for a few days, but then you must return to it to make a few changes.

- You need to have financial and technological resources. Even though you can start small, you are not going to last long if all you have is lunch money. When it comes to technological resources, you need to make sure that you have a steady access to the internet and the trading platform.

- You need to have financial discipline. You do not need to have a finance degree. Rather, you should be capable of understanding trends and numbers.

- You need to be emotionally strong. Things do not always go your way. But some of the biggest successes in Forex happen because people do not get emotional over their trades. They figure out ways to bounce back.

- You need to have the perseverance to always seek out new information, new ways to manage your risk, and look for new opportunities.

- Finally, you should be a sponge, able to absorb knowledge about the politics, economics, and market situations of a particular country. That means it is time to renew your newspaper subscriptions.

Why Choose Forex Over Other Options?

We just looked at the fact that Forex gives you a 24-hour market to work with. But what other benefits can we get by choosing Forex over other forms of security investments options?

Let us look into some benefits here.

Low Transaction Costs

For short-term traders, the Forex market is the best place to trade because of the low transaction cost. This is because of the over-the-counter structure that people can take advantage of. How is that possible? Well, you can use a purely electronic marketplace where you can interact directly with the market maker. This removes the need for any middlemen.

Let us take the example of an equity trader. Let us say that this trader has placed around 30 trades a day. For these trades, he has to pay around $20 in commission fees. Because of this, the trader then has to pay up to $600 simply as transaction costs every single day. This not only becomes a rather hefty investment, but it curbs profits and in some cases, creates losses. In an equity transaction, there are several people involved and this is why you usually end up paying a high transaction cost.

The Forex market is decentralized. There are no clearinghouses or exchanges. This means you do not have to spend unnecessarily on transaction fees.

Both The Bear and The Bull Are Profitable

The terms "bear" and "bull" are used to describe how markets are performing. This means they gauge whether a market is appreciating or depreciating in value and also describe investor sentiments about a market.

When the term "bull market" is used, it is referring to a market that is improving. In such scenarios, investors are optimistic about the fact that there will be an upward trend in the market for quite some time. The reason the word "bull" is used is because a bull typically attacks by lifting its horns up to sheesh-kebab its helpless victims.

On the other hand, the term "bear market" is used to describe a market in decline. When that happens, investors are pessimistic about the market's future. The word "bear" is used because a bear typically swipes down to attack.

When working on any other options other than Forex, you are going to be paying attention to market sentiments. It matters when you want to aim for a profitable return. In a Forex market, you do not have to worry whether the market is bull or bear because you are always buying one currency and selling another. This is why even a bear market is an opportunity.

Low Chances of Errors in Online Trades

When you are trading with currency, it generally involves a three-step process. You place your trade on the platform, the dealing desk at the Forex market executes your order (usually automatically), and then the trader receives the order confirmation logged onto his station. All of these steps are completed in a matter of a few seconds.

Now let us compare this with other trading options that have around five steps to complete your transaction. If you are the client, then you will be typically calling your broker to place a particular order. The broker then sends your order to the trading floor, where a specialist is responsible for matching the orders (this is done because there are many other brokers who might be competing for the same trade). Finally, the specialist confirms the order, and you receive a confirmation notification on your platform. As you can see, this is a pretty long process and the chances of something going wrong or human error taking over increases exponentially with each step.

Information is Key

We explored this point earlier but let us see what this means in more detail.

When you are dealing with currencies, you can analyze the countries. For example, do you want to discover the growth rate of countries? Then you should be looking at their GDP. Want to know about levels of production in a country? Then check out their industrial production data. By analyzing all of these facts, you get a picture of how a country is performing. This means that you can choose to invest in the currency of that country. There is an incredible amount of data released about a country, much more detailed and copious than the information about a company. This data cannot be falsified or adulterated. Everything is clear-cut for you to understand.

The Forex Market and How it Works

To better understand Forex, you need to know that the market involves a Forex quote, which is essentially the price of one currency in terms of another (because currencies are always traded in pairs). This means that one unit of the base currency matches the exchange rate of the quote currency.

Let us take an example. If you are dealing with EUR/USD and the trading value is at 1.13122, then it simply means that the price of 1 euro (which is the base currency) in dollars (which is the quote currency) is 1.13122 dollars.

We are going to look more into the basics of Forex in the next chapter, but for now, the idea of how the currency pairs are matched will help you understand future concepts.

Who Participates in the Forex Market?

When you examine it broadly, then there are 5 main participants in the Forex market. Most others can be placed in any of the 5 categories mentioned below.

Banks

One can say that banks are the major participants in the market. After all, we are dealing with currencies and their value is how commercial banks can assist with the nation's fiscal policies. At any given point in time, there are an average of 150 banks from around the world performing transactions in the Forex market.

It is important to know that banks do not only conduct transactions in the market on behalf of their customers but also on their own behalf with the sole aim of earning profits.

However, there is another group of banks that also participate in the Forex market: central banks. These banks have a direct impact on the Forex market because whatever policies or movements occur in the central banks, traders will pick up on that to check what is happening with the currencies they are trading. Additionally, central banks can also directly intervene in the market, leading to drastic shifts in currency values. For example, a central bank can use some of the reserves of its foreign and domestic currency reserves in order to buy foreign currencies in the market, thus influencing their value.

Brokers

Brokers are people who help arrange trades between two or multiple dealers. They constantly monitor the currency rates and fluctuations so that they can offer some of the best avenues of investment for their clients. Brokers do not invest their own money. They are simply people who arrange for transactions to take place.

Multinational Corporations

When MNCs deal with international operations, they make use of the Forex market. This happens specifically during the process of imports and exports when the multinational companies have to convert their money in order to pay for the transactions. Some MNCs even have their own floors in the market with designated traders who help make more profits and minimize the risk involved in the exchange rates.

Individual Investors

With the level of convenience and accessibility available to people around the world, individual traders have been flocking to the Forex market like people rushing to the electronics store on a Black Friday weekend. And you are going to be joining the platform as well. The only difference is, you will be better informed than most people.

Small Businesses

When it comes to managing cash flow on an international level, then the task becomes challenging for small businesses. What rules do they adhere to? How can they conduct a transaction while being completely aware of currency exchange rates? By using Forex, SMEs can leverage the currency information readily available on the platform and also hedge currency risk. When SMEs begin to deal with transactions on an international level, one of the biggest challenges that they face is currency risk. In order to either minimize or eliminate the currency risk, they use a process called hedging where they will lock in on an exchange rate today. When they conduct transactions in the future, they will be using the locked-in currency exchange rate and not whatever rate is present at the time of the transaction. This way, even if the value of their currency drops in the future, they are not going to risk facing the repercussions of it. They have already locked their exchange rate.

What's in It For You?

Another way to ask that question: is Forex profitable?

The short answer is that yes, it is profitable. The long answer is that there is no easy way to make profits.

Many people enter the Forex market thinking that they are not going to make the same mistakes as someone else, only to end up losing their investments and feeling like they were swindled.

But Forex is about big risks and big rewards.

In fact, one of the biggest roles that you will be adopting while working in Forex is risk management. You need to be constantly thinking about the options you will take to mitigate a specific risk and what strategies you will utilize. If you are trying to risk too much in a trade in order to make sure you can face losses in the future, then you are going to find yourself exiting Forex faster than you can say "risky business".

Here is something that most traders don't realize when they enter Forex: you have to expect losses.

You might experience losses in a single day, over multiple days, or even across weeks. Those are the situations that every trader must face because the end goal is to make profits over the long-term.

This is why you need to enter Forex with proper control over your emotions and the right frame of mind. We are going to explore this further in the coming chapters, but for now, you need to know this: you have to be prepared for the Forex market.

Remember this, at the end of the day, you are going to be making the decisions that will dictate the direction of your trades. When things do not look good, Forex traders often end up blaming the government, the trading platform, luck, God, the fate of the universe, or whatever else they can find to blame. But the end result is that they are the ones who take the final actions. Sometimes it pays off and at other times, it may not.

However, there are a few steps you can take to give you an edge in the market. One of them is choosing your broker. Whatever trading platform you choose, make sure that you have done your research about that platform. Giving you numerous features and speedy execution of trades is important, but at the same time, they need to provide you with honesty and transparency as well. You should also ideally choose a broker who can provide a demo account.

With a demo account, you can paper trade (demo trade). Take advantage of it and practice your demo trades. Make as many mistakes as you can. Learn how to work the system properly. You need to reach a point where you should be getting consistent results over the long-term. Once you have found your strategy, you can implement it in real trades.

Are there any other tricks or information that could be useful for you?

Of course there are. We are going to look at all of them. From the basics that you need to be aware of before starting your trade to getting into the mindset of a winner, you are going to get an edge over others in the market.

Chapter 2: The Basics that Everyone Needs to Know Before They Start

Where Do You Trade Forex?

To trade in Forex, you are going to be using special platforms that are essentially labeled as "brokers". This is why there was an emphasis on choosing the right broker as this can impact how effectively you trade and how much knowledge you are privy to at any point.

Additionally, you should be picking your broker based on the strategy you are using in Forex (discussed further). For some strategies, you need to have low spreads and speedy executions while for other strategies that are focused on the long-term, you might need to focus on swapping. When you evaluate platforms, you will find out that some are better than others not because of the overall features, but mainly due to the suitability of the platform to your strategies.

When you have matched the broker to the strategy, look for some additional features that you can get from the platform as well. These don't change the way you work on the platforms but simply provide you with convenience.

Finally, do check if your broker is regulated in its home country. This allows you to check that they are following a certain set of criteria and requirements, which is important to make sure that they are not going to break rules during their operation.

What Exactly is a Currency Pair?

A currency pair, in essence, is a quote. You are being quoted one currency against the other. In such a manner, you are comparing the value of one currency against the other. When you discover that the value of one currency appreciates, you then conduct a sale to net yourself some profits.

When you are trading with currencies, you are using "contracts". The contracts are essentially lot sizes of the units of currency that you are going to purchase. Typically, the usual contract or lot size is 100,000. This means that you are going to purchase 100,000 units of a particular currency. But many trading firms and platforms also offer what are known as mini lots (which have a size of 10,000 units) and micro lots (which have a unit size of 1,000).

Now let us see how this works and how you typically make a profit with an example.

Since we have familiarized ourselves with the EUR/USD pair, we are going to use it for our example here. Let us imagine that the exchange rate of EUR/USD is 1.13 and you have made a purchase of 10,000 units of euros. What this means is that each euro is equivalent to $1.13. You have spent $11,300 to purchase 10,000 units of euros (10,000 x 1.13).

You have all these units of euros with you and you decide to wait. After two weeks, you notice that the value of the euro has appreciated. The EUR/USD is now going for 1.2, or in other words, one euro is now equivalent to $1.2. At this point, you decide that you are going to sell the units of euros that you have with you.

What happens now?

Well, you exchange the euros and receive $12,000 in return (10,000 x 1.2).

You made a profit of $700 on your trade.

Of course, the reality is not as simple as that. If it was, then we would have a lot more people striking it rich on the platform and a lot more Ferraris rolling down our neighborhood.

However, that example gives you the gist of what you can expect from a Forex trade.

The Basic Terms of the Forex Market

Now that you are ready to become a trader, you should also learn some of the Forex lingo that you are going to come across.

In other words, time to walk the walk and talk the talk.

Long/Short

When you have a currency pair with you, then you have an important decision to make. Are you going to buy that currency pair or sell it?

If you are aiming to buy the currency pair, then you are hoping that the base currency increases in value so that you can sell it at a profit in the future.

In trading long, this action is commonly referred to as "taking the long position" or "going long". Traders usually shorten it to "long".

When you sell, then what you are doing is that you are selling the base currency in the hopes that it decreases in value at a future date. This way, you can buy it back and make a profit out of it.

Trading lingo refers to this action as "taking a short position" or "going short". In short, it is called "short" (see what we did there?).

The best way to remember the above terms is to know this:

- Buy = long

- Sell = short

Pip? Pipettes? What the Pip Are They?

It is recommended that you take your time to digest the information presented here. This is truly important if you would like to understand what the values of the currencies mean. Even a slight shift in the currencies can affect the trade.

When there is a change in the value between the currency pairs, then that change is expressed as a "pip".

For example, let us take an earlier example and say that 1 euro = 1.1388 U.S. dollars. After a couple of days, you see a change in the value; it has risen to 1.1389. That 0.0001 rise in the value of the currency is called "1 pip".

That is why the pip usually indicates the last decimal in a currency exchange value. Usually, you see currencies expressed to a maximum of four decimal places, but there are exceptions to the rule. One such exception is the Japanese yen, which is shown up to two decimal places.

So if a 1 pip increase in the value of a U.S. dollar is shown as 0.0001, then the same pip value is shown as 0.01 for the Japanese yen.

Still confused? Let's try and use an example.

Let's see what we know so far.

1 euro = 1.1388 U.S. dollars.

However, for the Japanese yen: 1 euro = 122.26 yen.

The currency itself is expressed up to two decimal places. Now if there was a rise in value by one pip, then the new exchange rate would be:

1 euro = 122.27 yen.

Which brings us to pipettes.

On some platforms and for certain brokers, currencies are not represented using the standard 4 and 2 decimal place positions. Rather, they are expressed up to 5 or 3 decimal places.

This means that the EUR/USD will be: 1 euro = 1.13886 U.S. dollars.

Similarly, EUR/JPY (where JPY is the Japanese yen) will be expressed as: 1 euro = 122.278 Japanese yen.

When you use the above format, then an increase in a single value is no longer referred to as a pip. It will become a fraction of a pip or a "pipette".

Thus, an increase in value by 1 pip will be shown as 0.0001 or 0.01, depending on the currency, while an increase in value by 1 pipette is shown as 0.00001 or 0.001, depending on the currency.

So how can you use these terms to express the currencies you are dealing with? It's simple.

Let us take this example:

1 euro = 1.13886 U.S. dollars.

With the above currency, you have (starting from the right at 6 and moving to the left):

- 6 pipettes
- 8 pips
- 80 pips
- 300 pips
- 1,000 pips
- 10,000 pips

Therefore, if the value increases from 1.13886 dollars to 1.13986, then the change in the value is 10 pips.

Now comes the rather complicated part of measuring the value of each pip. How can we do that? Well, we use the below formula:

The change in the value of the quote currency x current exchange rate = value of the pip in the base currency.

Time for another example and this time, let's see something other than EUR/USD. We will use GBP/USD (British pounds and U.S. dollars).

Let us assume that GBP/USD = 1.27299.

We are now going to calculate the value of 1 pip.

What do we know so far?

- 1 pip = 0.0001

- 1 British pound= 1.27299 U.S. dollars

We simply add the information above into the formula. We get:

0.0001 x 1/1.27299 = value of the pip in base currency.

In other words, 1 pip = 0.000127299 USD

Why is it so important to calculate the pip value? Simple, it expresses the shift in the value of your lot size.

Let us imagine that you have purchased 1,000 units of GBP/USD. Then you calculate the shift in lot value by multiplying the pip value by the number of lots you have with you. This is translated as:

1,000 x 0.000127299 = 0.127299 USD.

This means that every time the value of the currency pair changes by 1 pip, the value of your lot size changes by 0.127299 USD. Therefore, if your currency increases by 8 pips, then you have made a profit of 1.018392 USD (8 x 0.127299 USD).

This little calculation helps you keep track of your investment, find out patterns, and strategize for the future more effectively.

The Bid, The Ask, and The Spread

When you are given a quote in Forex, you are provided with two prices: the bid price and the ask price.

Basically, the bid price refers to the amount your broker is willing to pay to purchase the base currency for the quote currency.

The ask price on the other hand simply refers to the price at which your broker will sell the base currency.

Usually, the bid price is lower than the ask price, but that is not always the case.

Now let's look at it with an example.

EUR/USD:

- Selling price = 1.1257

- Buying price = 1.1240

So we know that the bid price is the buying rate of the broker. So guess which of the above two numbers is the bid price?

If you guessed that the "buying price" is the bid price, then you are wrong.

Using the numbers above, you have to understand that the "Selling price" refers to the amount at which *you* are going to sell to the broker (a.k.a. the *buying price* of the broker).

It could get confusing if you did not know about the distinction between the two prices. It is always recommended that you take some time to just look at the selling price and buying price of currencies to figure out the bid and ask price of the brokers. This helps you get comfortable with the numbers to a point where you can easily make connections on your platform and you won't forget what you are supposed to be looking at when someone says "bid price".

Finally, we come to the term "spread". When someone mentions this term, then you are looking at the difference between the bid and the ask price.

Let's take a moment to do a quick recap.

EUR/USD

1.1257/1.1240

Base currency = EUR

Quote currency = USD

Bid price = 1.1257

Ask price = 1.1240

Spread = 17 pips (1.1257 - 1.1240)

Margin

When you are trading in Forex, you are required to set a "Margin". This term refers to the minimum deposit or collateral that you are going to place for your trades.

When you set your margin, you will be able to understand what size loan you can take so that you can access a larger amount of capital.

Leverage

A trader uses the term "leverage" to define how much of the loan he or she can use in order to receive a boost in trading capital. Because you are increasing your capital, you not only increase your profits but even your losses exponentially. This is why most trading platforms will provide you with advice on your margin and leverage. If they don't, then you are on the wrong platform!

Stop-loss Order

Simply put, a stop-loss order is a limit or condition placed the trader to commit to a sell action when the order reaches a certain point or price. You typically give the stop-loss order to your broker and they do the rest. A trader usually develops a stop-loss order when he or she would like to minimize the loss that they incur on a particular trade. This is useful when traders are unable to monitor the progress of the currency for a long time or they have to step away from their platform. It allows them to avoid any unexpected surprises.

Elements That Affect the Forex Market

When you are trading in Forex, then you must be aware of certain factors that affect the market. Being aware of these factors or elements helps you stay ahead of the game and look for the right information to gain an advantage in your trade.

Interest Rates

When there is an increase in the interest rate of a country's currency, then there is an appreciation in the value of the currency. This is because it provides money lenders with higher rates to work with, which in turn attracts more foreign investment. The culmination of this process is an increase in the exchange rate of the currencies.

Inflation

In typical circumstances, when a country consistently has a low rate of inflation, then that is an indication that the country's currency value is rising. The opposite is true for those countries whose inflation rates rise at unexpected levels.

Public Debt

When nations have high debts or public deficits, then they become unattractive in the eyes of foreign investors. When a country has a large debt, then there is a potential for high inflation rates. In many cases, the government has to manage the debts and to do so, they will end up increasing the supply of money. However, this has consequences as increasing money supply results in high inflation. In other words, it shows that the country is unable to manage its deficits by relying on domestic factors. This, in turn, shows instability within the country. Additionally, when countries are in debt for a long time, then investors become apprehensive, thinking that if the country cannot make due on their obligations, then what are the chances for investors to receive their money?

Eventually, their currency value drops and you might notice it in the Forex market.

Trade Terms

Trade is an important indicator of a country's financial situation. If the rate of a country's exports increases much higher than its rate of imports, then it is an indication that there are more favorable terms of trade. Foreign nations are always looking for trade terms that are favorable to them. When this happens, the demand for the exports of the host country increases. This increases revenue, which increases the demand for the currency of that country. Eventually, this demand is reflected in the Forex market in the form of increasing values.

Economic Performance

This is probably one of the more obvious factors that affect the currency in a Forex market. When the economic performance of the country improves, then more and more investors are ready to spend their capital in the country. Other countries who provide higher risks for investors will find that their foreign investments reduce.

Chapter 3: The Foreign Exchange: What Will You Really Trade?

Money, Money, Money: A Brief History

It all started with chaos.

Currency exchange has been in place for a long time now. And by a long time, we are not talking about a couple of hundred years or even a few thousand years. We are referring to the BC period. More specifically, to around 10,000 BC. The only difference was that at that time people used the barter system to exchange goods and services. But this created feelings of dissatisfaction among the traders. How can one gauge the value of objects? Even if they were referring to a specific object, how can they say that the object from one place is better than another? For example, let us assume that you were providing two bags of rice for a fine carpet. (I''m not sure if this was the exchange rate, but let's pretend that it is. Though if you are giving two bags of rice for a carpet, then that carpet better fly!) Now, you know that in your little village or town, carpets are of the finest quality. But does that mean all the carpets around the world have the same quality? Does that mean you are getting a fair return for your two bags of rice? Now imagine this scenario playing out between the countries. How can one set accurate values for each country's "currencies"? How can exchanges take place that are fair and governed by the right rules?

This situation created a system of bias and prejudice. This started to disrupt whatever form of economy was used during those times.

Eventually, the earliest coins were made in parts of what we now refer to as Turkey. Empires and nations around the world began to manufacture their own coins using precious materials like gold and silver.

This controlled the chaos of exchanges that took place between traders because everything had a proper value. If you are going to purchase something, you knew how much you had to pay for it.

Fast forward to the 19th century. More specifically, to the year 1847. Up until now, countries were commonly utilizing gold and silver to make international payments. But that changed with the introduction of the Gold Standard Monetary System. With this system in place, the paper currencies of the countries had a value directly linked to gold. This means that a certain value of money from a country could be converted into a specific amount of gold, depending on that country's currency value.

Over time, this system was dropped in order to give each country a degree of autonomy when managing their affairs. This means that each country is responsible for creating their own currencies without leveraging it against anything. When governments began issuing their own paper currencies that were not attached to a physical commodity like gold or silver, that currency was given the term "fiat money".

Why is this significant? As we had seen, autonomy.

But once again, what does this actually mean?

With the presence of fiat money, the value of the money is dependant on the relationship between the supply and demand of the country along with the stability of the government. Rather than using gold and silver to decide the value of the money, the situation of the country would derive the value of the money.

Enter World War II.

And once again, it started with chaos.

The whole world was experiencing unprecedented levels of chaos. Governments were scrambling to find a solution to stabilize the economies of the world. They turned their eyes to the U.S. dollar.

In order to provide a solution, the Bretton Woods Agreement was established. According to this agreement, the U.S. dollar was set as the exchange rate for gold, giving nations around the world one currency to work with when managing international trades. Other currencies were eventually pegged against the U.S. dollar.

Once again, another solution to control the chaos of exchanges was formed. But did it last? Sadly, no.

History has a strange habit of repeating itself. Because even the Bretton Woods Agreement became obsolete as it became apparent that countries progressed at different speeds. In fact, it was observed that new rules introduced in countries could change trade laws and currency values.

In 1971, the Bretton Woods Agreement was dropped. The world needed a different system of currency valuation.

The U.S. was once again placed in the pilot seat and with the country's guidance, a free-floating market was introduced that would actually determine the *exchange value* of currencies based on the demand and supply in a particular country.

Of course, this innovative way of looking at currencies brought with it a whole new set of problems, the most prominent being the fact that it was not always easy to establish fair exchange rates. Additionally, gathering information about a country and its governmental policies, domestic situations, and trade policies could not be done quickly enough.

Then came the 1990s, a time we should all be thankful for. After all, it was because of the internet boom that we now have access to Facebook, online multiplayer RPGs, Netflix, and YouTube.

One of the greatest achievements of the internet was the availability of information instantly to anyone, anywhere in the world. The foundation provided by the internet allowed people to create new and innovative technologies.

These innovations led to the establishment of various trading platforms.

As we saw earlier, prior to the availability of trading platforms, the Forex market was simply something only certain entities or individuals with high net worth could access. It was never really available to everyone and the thought of joining it probably meant you had to have a million dollars, take a loan, perform an ancient ritual to the god of money, and maybe even sacrifice a few goats.

It was like a realm that everyone wanted to be in but no one had any access to.

But trading platforms changed all that. Because of these platforms, there was a paradigm shift in the way people approached the Forex market.

This brings us to the concept of institutional and retail trading.

Institutional Versus Retail Trading

In the world of trading, there are basically two forms of traders: institutional and retail. The difference between them dictates the way they approach their trades. For example, institutional traders usually make large trades as compared to retail traders. But what are they exactly?

Their names might just give you a clue as to what you can understand about them.

Retail traders refers to individual traders. These traders can be anyone in the world who has the ability to get in on a trade. On the other hand, institutional traders are those who represent large financial institutions, hedge funds, banks, or other big firms that manage money. You could say that institutional traders are "corporate" traders whereas retail traders are "home" traders.

So does the amount invested in the trade dictate the type of trader one becomes? Is that the only point of distinction?

Not quite.

Analysis

A retail trader usually prefers to use some sort of technical analysis system for their trades. They utilize price patterns and behaviors in the past or indicators in the present that dictate future price scenarios. On the other hand, institutional traders do not usually refer to only technical patterns or systems to show them opportunities in their trade.

Focus

As institutional traders have been dealing with the system for a long time, their experience has led them to hone their skills well. They make use of market sentiments and fundamentals. They make use of trading psychology (which is a firm grasp on their emotions and keeping an analytical mind despite the situation) and understanding of overall responses towards a currency. They are keeping a close eye on the news to see if there are certain trends or reactions that they can pick up on.

Retail traders are not experienced in managing risks or having a proper psychological mind for trading. However, this is a situation that happens to everyone who gets started in Forex trading. No one can be prepared for what they will experience. They have to experience it first before they can decide how to keep their minds sharp.

Leverage

Institutional traders do not usually use leverage. Their main attention is spent on risk management. Even if a situation were to occur where they had to make use of leverages, they would be careful about how much leverage they are going to use.

On the other hand, retail traders make the mistake of looking for brokers that provide them with high leverages. While that act in itself is not wrong, it does pose a problem to those retailers who choose their brokers solely on the criteria of how much leverage those brokers provide them.

Now that we have understood more about the Forex market and its players, it is time we look at the most essential component of the market, currencies. More importantly, we are going to look at some of the major players in the Forex market.

Popular Currencies

U.S. Dollar

The U.S. dollar is combined with numerous currencies to either form the base or quote currency. Some of the combinations involve:

- USD/JPY (Japanese yen)

- USD/CAD (Canadian dollar)

- USD/CHF (Swiss franc)

- EUR/USD (Euro, but you already knew that with the number of times we have used this in our examples. It wouldn't be surprising if this will be the first pair your trade in.)

- GBP/USD (British pound)

- AUD/USD (Australian dollar)

- NZD/USD (New Zealand dollar)

The U.S. dollar becomes the base currency when used in exotic pairs (and by exotic, we are referring to the fact that these combinations are not very common on the trading platform). These currencies include the below:

- SEK (Swedish krona)

- SGD (Singapore dollar)

- NOK (Norwegian krone)

- DKK (Danish krone)

- MXN (Mexican peso)

- BRL (Brazilian real)

- ZAR (South African rand)

The U.S. dollar is also considered the standard currency unit that is used in many of the commodity markets around the world (especially in the crude oil and gold markets). Currently, it also takes the important position of being the most employed reserve currency in the world. These features of the U.S. dollar allows it to have trade deficits with many countries in the world without facing the problem of depreciation.

Because the economy of the US has a strong influence on the rest of the world the volatility of the currency ranges from low to medium. Because of its market orientation, many corporations and business lead their decision-making processes using the US dollar.

Euro

The Euro becomes the base or quote currency when included in the below pairs:

- EUR/GBP
- EUR/AUD
- EUR/USD
- EUR/NZD
- EUR/CHF
- EUR/CAD

- EUR/JPY

It solely becomes the base currency when you pair it with the following currencies:

- SEK

- NOK

- CNY (Chinese yuan)

- DKK

- MXN

- BRL

- ZAR

- SGD

After the Euro was formed in the year 1999 and then officially implemented in 2002, it quickly became fairly commonly used in most of the countries of the European Union (EU).

One of the main reasons for bringing about the implementation of the euro was to make sure that there was easy free trade between the member countries of the Eurozone. It was also set up to boost public relations and political integration.

The currency pair EUR/USD is commonly referred to as "fiber". This is because the Eurozone includes the greatest fiber optic network in the world.

The Central banks of the member countries of the EU along with the European Central Bank (ECB) form policies and rules to manage the currency. The euro is managed through the European System of Central Banks (ESCB).

The power to make monetary policies concerning the euro lies with the ECB only. However, other members of the ESCB also have the ability to issue and then distribute the coins and notes of the currency. Because the euro has been adopted by numerous countries, the Eurozone has been able to become one of the largest economies in the world. For this reason, the euro is a stronger currency than the U.S. dollar.

Australian Dollar

The Australian dollar becomes the base or quote currency in the following pairs:

- AUD/CAD

- GBP/AUD

- EUR/AUD

- AUD/CHF

- AUD/JPY

- AUD/NZD

- AUD/USD

It becomes the base currency along with a few exotic currencies. However, it is not as popular with other currencies as the U.S. dollar and euro.

In the world of trading, the Australian dollar or AUD is also known as "Aussie". This nickname is also used when it is paired with the U.S. dollar in AUD/USD. In the Forex market, it is the 6th most traded currency and also amounts to nearly 5% of the foreign exchange transactions conducted around the world.

One of the reasons why the currency is so popular is the fact that the intervention from the Australian government in the Forex market is practically nonexistent. Add to that the fact there is usually stability in the politics and economics of Australia, and you have a currency with low volatility.

Canadian Dollar

The Canadian dollar becomes the base or quote currency in the following pairs:

- GBP/CAD
- EUR/CAD
- AUD/CAD
- NZD/CAD
- CAD/JPY
- USD/CAD

- CAD/CHF

The Canadian dollar, or CAD, is also commonly referred to as "loonie". The nickname is also used when it forms a pair with the U.S. dollar to create the USD/CAD. The use of the nickname is due to the fact that there is an image of a loon (which is a form of aquatic bird) on the face of the currency note.

One of the notable features of the Canadian economy is how similar it is to the United States in many ways. For example, it is mostly production - and market - oriented. It has also evolved a lot since World War II, mainly focusing on being industrial. It also pays heavy attention to its mining, manufacturing, and service sectors.

British Pound

The British pound sterling, or the GBP, forms the base or quote currency in the following pairs:

- GBP/CAD

- GBP/AUD

- GBP/NZD

- EUR/GBP

- GBP/CHF

- GBP/USD

- GBP/JPY

It also becomes the base currency with few of the other exotic currencies in the world such as the ones below:

- BRL

- DKK

- CNY

- MXN

- ZAR

- SGD

- SEK

- NOK

The GBP is one of the most widely traded currencies in the world, along with the U.S. dollar, the euro, and the Japanese yen. Of the major currencies in the world, the GBP has the highest value. When paired with the U.S. dollar to form the GBP/USD, the pair is given the nickname "cable". This is mainly due to the fact that, at one point, the rates of the currency pair were transmitted using the trans-Atlantic cable.

Japanese Yen

The Japanese yen, or the JPY, forms the base or quote currency in the following pairs:

- NZD/JPY
- AUD/JPY
- EUR/JPY
- USD/JPY
- CAD/JPY
- CHF/JPY
- GBP/JPY

The Japanese yen was originally pegged to the U.S. dollar at the end of World War II, but that was changed in the year 1971. The Japanese economy mainly revolves around the manufacturing industry. Initially, the currency of Japan had been weak because it was mainly circulated within its borders. This restriction in its currency prevented it from attaining a favorable position in foreign trade. Eventually, the rise in industrial production and the increase in foreign investments in other countries have given it an edge.

Swiss Franc

The Swiss franc, or CHF, forms the base or quote currency in the following pairs:

- NZD/CHF
- AUD/CHF
- CAD/CHF
- GBP/CHF

- EUR/CHF

- CHF/JPY

- USD/CHF

The first thing that people notice about the Swiss franc is the initials of the currency. CHF is used to denote the currency because it stands for "Confederatio Helvetica Franc". Although the currency does not have a nickname when it stands on its own, it does have a nickname when in pair with the U.S. dollar. The USD/CHF pair is commonly referred to as the "Swissie".

One of the most attractive features of the Swiss franc is that it is a rather stable currency. This is because of Switzerland's political and economic stability. Additionally, the currency is mostly used as a form of reserve currency by numerous financial institutions and individuals who are highly wealthy.

New Zealand Dollar

The New Zealand dollar, or the NZD, forms the base or quote currency in the following pairs:

- NZD/CAD
- NZD/CHF
- EUR/NZD
- GBP/NZD
- NZD/JPY
- NZD/USD

Informally, the currency is also referred to as "kiwi" by traders because of the fact that a picture of a kiwi appears on the $1 coin. Additionally, traders also use the nickname to refer to the NZD/USD pair. Typically, the New Zealand dollar's validity hovers in the low to medium levels.

New Zealand and Australia share the same change in direction for their economy. Initially, the country was dependent on its agriculture market which was limited to British concessionaires. It then shifted its focus to becoming a free and industrialized market whose presence is felt all over the globe and is even going toe-to-toe with some of the big economies. One of the things that set New Zealand apart is that despite the improvements in technology, the country still has a large percentage of agricultural exports.

With all the focus on the market, trade, and currencies, there is still another vital cog in this machine, you. That is why, in the next chapter, we are going to focus on helping you think like a winner.

Chapter 4 - The Mindset of a Winner: What They Do and How They Do It

By now, you are slowly getting a picture of the complex world of Forex trading. You have probably understood that there is more to it than just putting all your money in one place and returning to it at a later time, hoping that your money has doubled or maybe quadrupled in size.

Here is the truth: what you have read is just the tip of the iceberg. There is a lot more ground to cover.

Which is why, before going any further, it is important to cover one vital component in all of this.

You.

You Are Not Other Forex Traders

Remember how we compared institutional traders and retail traders? When you look at the traits that retail traders carry with themselves, you might realize that those are probably the ways new traders, or "newbies", would work.

You might be doing the same.

And that is completely alright. You need to get a feel for the system. You might figure out a few things on your own, while others might require some prompts and assistance from other sources. But there are certain characteristics of other traders that are best not adopted. Let us look at a few of them.

The Blame Game

One of the things that a lot of beginner traders do is blame the market for any unfortunate circumstances. It takes a lot to admit that you have made a mistake. Because you see, the market is just numbers. It was not designed to predict your mind and make sure you fail. It's not a Jedi.

Take a lesson from the workings of institutional traders. They always analyze the market. When things do not go their way, they start figuring out the solution to the problem. That should be your focus as well.

Track Record

One of the important things to note is that, as much as money is the end game, it should not always be the intent of your trading. It is equally important to maintain a good track record. You cannot hope to continue to trade when you are afraid of losing what money you have. Forex involves great risks and you need the necessary capital for it. In the case of institutional traders, they have the right financial backing, so they can shrug off a loss and move on to the next plan.

But how can you gain capital without taking a loan or leveraging your account?

Easy, you keep a healthy track record. You will soon be able to accumulate capital for bigger trades.

Risk Within Your Limits

When you are managing your risk, one of the important questions that you will be asking yourself is, just how much capital can I risk for each trade?

Ideally, you should not risk more than 1% of your capital on a single trade. This serves two purposes:

- If you encounter a loss it won't put a huge dent in your capital.

- You will be able to learn valuable lessons from the trade and have enough capital to try new strategies on different trades.

News is Facts, Not Prediction

It is tempting to feel that you can make a prediction and profit from it based on what news information you have. But the reality of the situation is different.

In the wake of economic releases, you might find that currency values can either rise or fall. At that moment, it becomes tempting to anticipate the direction the pair will move and trade accordingly. Seems like a sure way to nab an easy quarter of a million dollars.

But that is a big mistake. The news is simply providing you with the latest information. Do not anticipate what direction the news will take the market. Rather, create a strategy that you can use to trade after the news comes out.

No Plan. No Trade.

You need to make sure that you have a trading plan prepared for yourself. Essentially, this is a document that you have written or created that gives a direction for your strategy. It lets you know what, how, and when you day trade in the Forex market.

When you create this plan, make sure it includes suggestions for the type of currencies you should trade, what time you will conduct your trade, and what time of the day you have allotted for analyzing your trades or for conducting research.

Additionally, you should also cover all the rules you have for risk management. You should be able to tell how you are able to enter and exit the trades.

When You Are Starting, Forget Fundamental Analysis

Despite what many people might think, do not focus on economic or fundamental analysis. You are starting out. Your first priority is to get used to the lay of the land.

In many cases, traders get caught up in the news. This compels them to form certain biases about trades, especially when they watch or read information that claims that the economic situation of a country is good or bad.

Remember this: when you are day trading, forget the long-term repercussions and outlook. Your mission, should you choose to accept (and you probably should), is to focus on implementing your strategy effectively. This message will not self-destruct in 5 seconds (we still have a lot of topics to cover).

This does not mean that fundamental analysis is not preferable. In fact, quite the opposite: fundamental analysis plays an extremely vital role in trading. But you need to first begin by gaining a sense of mastery over one form of analysis.

In the short-run, good investments can go bad and bad investments can turn around. When you have long-term biases, you tend to move away from your trading strategy and simply shifting to a new strategy is like nosediving into loss territory without a parachute.

Emotional Wreck

If you cannot keep your emotions in check, then you are on a path to destroy everything you have built during your trades. Successful traders understand how to manage their frustrations and their temper, knowing full well that any hasty decision taken in the "heat of the moment" is only going to create further problems.

There are many ways you can keep your emotions in check. However, today we shall try and examine this from another perspective.

We are going to learn how to build your confidence and in turn, explain how you can manage your emotions.

Step 1: Be Disciplined

Remember that we just talked about all the things that other traders often do that you should probably not be doing.

One of the things that is common among traders is the lack of discipline. Most traders are not brilliant. They are not the people in the movies who can perform quick calculations in their mind as though they have a Mac operating system installed in their brain.

In real life, the most successful traders are those who have discipline. Take bank traders for example.

In banks, traders usually work under a risk manager. It is the job of the risk manager to make sure that the bank traders know the boundaries within which they should operate.

These bank traders follow one fundamental rule: they are not allowed to take on more risks than they are granted. Each trader is given a specific number or amount. All risks must be below the number specified. The risk manager is present to oversee the risks taken by the traders. If a trader exceeds the amount mentioned, then he or she is given a single warning. If the trader repeats the error again, he or she is fired.

Here is a surprising fact: even traders who bring in millions of dollars to the bank are shown the door if they mess with this rule.

We do not have risk managers in our lives (unless you can afford one). But we do have risk management capabilities.

Step 2: Change Your Beliefs

Your belief system is what establishes, to an extent, your mental fitness. These beliefs tune your attention toward a specific idea and change your attitude towards the things that surround you. They help you figure out how to deal with life's many components.

But most importantly, they help you form your emotions.

You can agree or disagree with a certain idea or point of view. You determine if something is right or wrong based on your beliefs. But here is a question that needs to be asked: how many of these beliefs are helping you see the bigger picture or, even more importantly, the right picture?

Psychology has identified a tendency in human beings called confirmation bias. According to this bias, people generally look for ideas and facts that confirm their viewpoints and ignore everything else that opposes them. In other words, they seek out facts to confirm what they already believe, even though the same people claim to be objective. In fact, if you go ahead and check your browser history, you might find some traces of confirmation bias. In many cases, even though we look for contradictory ideas, we generally find more information that supports our theories, suppositions, and viewpoints than opposing ideas.

Having confirmation bias is harmless when it comes to supporting your favorite music genre or explaining which Teenage Mutant Ninja Turtle is the best (Donatello for the win, by the way).

But when it comes to Forex, having confirmation bias is not just folly, it's perilous.

When you have flexible beliefs, you will approach a situation with an analytical mind. You will see every mistake as a learning experience and losing trades as lessons. Instead of feeling disappointed, angry, or frustrated, you will be focused on getting better.

Step 3: Evaluate Your Mistakes

But you should not stop simply at your beliefs. Once you have entered into the right frame of mind, it is time to focus it in the right direction.

Examine the situation that led to the loss. Identify what mistake was made. Consult with your broker and other traders if you have to.

You should be able to understand what happened, what conditions led to the loss, why you did or did not take a particular action. Were you following your strategy? Did you break any of the rules you have established for your plan?

If you made a successful trade, then you should look for the steps that led to that success. When you examine both your successes and failures, you will be able to make connections that teach you how to proceed further in Forex.

Step 4: Write Down the Consequences

Your mistakes have consequences and you need to be aware of them. Make a list of the consequences, both bad and good. This helps remind you what steps you should not be taking in future trades and why.

Step 5: Create an Action Plan

At this point, you are ready to create a different approach to your trading. Remember this: every mistake is an opportunity to create a trading success. The more mistakes you make, the more clearly defined your next course of action will be until all you have is a path that helps you get to your next success.

If you realize that the mistake comes from your strategy, then redefine and refine the strategy. Work on it until you are able to employ it without committing any errors.

Step 6: Master Your Stress and Confusion

Just google stress management and you will be bombarded with a horde of self-help books, systems, stress management gurus, and indicators.

Eventually, you have traders equipping themselves with multi-screen monitors, fast computers, the latest software, and abundant data. And does that help them?

Nope.

It's like someone with no knowledge of tech found the Iron Man suit of armor and is now tasked with going mano-a-mano against Thanos.

Exactly. Time to count your prayers because you are going to get snapped into oblivion.

It is not about what equipment you have. That hardly matters when you haven't even reached the root cause of what might be compelling you to make mistakes: your own stress and confusion.

In fact, have you ever gone on YouTube and seen those ads where this guy pops up claiming that he can get you earning millions in just a short time using a secret technique that has a fancy name? None of those work. Think about it, if people really knew the secret to earning millions (or if anyone did), would they actually go on sharing it to get *more* money? In fact, would they actually have a subscription model or high product prices?

This is what happens to people who are under a lot of stress or who get confused; they begin to look for alternatives and fall prey to any advertising.

What you should be doing is studying your own techniques and strategies. If you feel like things are getting overwhelming, do not go ahead and make another trade. Take a short break until you can figure out what is causing your stress and disappointment.

Was it a loss that you did not expect? Then focus on what caused that loss.

What is a sudden shift in the market? Find out how and why that shift happened. Discover methods to predict that shift in the future.

Incorrect news and information? Change the channel!

Commonly Used Platforms for Day Trading

To have the right trade, you need to have the right tools. These usually come in the form of the trading platform you utilize for your trades. We have compiled a few that are not just popular but recommended by many traders around the world.

TD Ameritrade

One of the most attractive features of this platform is the ability to stream news, giving you more power over the information you would like to receive. The platform also provides you with numerous educational materials made to help you get started on the trading platform. You can use its "Social Signals" feature, which extracts information about your trades from Twitter. These tweets could be from other experienced traders or industry experts as well.

Fidelity Investments

Fidelity is known to have one of the best trade-routing systems, which helps provide their customers with lower trade costs when compared to most platforms.

The platform has technology integrated into its operation to make sure that there is a visible improvement on orders placed by customers. This gives the customers on the platform the ability to make a "Buy" trade at a considerably lower price than shown in the market. Additionally, it also allows traders to commit to a "Sell" option at a slightly higher price.

The whole platform is easy to navigate and might we also add, rather aesthetically pleasing.

You even have educational materials and features, such as tax planning, to help you with your trades. You can examine your financial health by connecting to outside accounts on other platforms.

IG

IG has been setting up to become one
of the most trusted and regulated
platforms for trading around the globe.
You are able to make use of their real-
time exchange data to power up your
research and trading. IG is also used to
publicly trade in many of the countries
around the world. Because of this global
presence, there are proper jurisdictions
and regulations that they adhere to. As
their platform keeps on improving, IG
manages to add in more features to
ensure that traders have commission-
based spreads in the Forex market.

CMC Markets

Founded in 1989, CMC Markets is a
popular trading platform in the UK that
is now making its presence known
around the world. It is also listed in the
London Stock Exchange, which means it
provides you with a layer of transparency.
When using the platform, you might as

well be spoilt for choice as it offers you 300+ currency pairs to choose from.

You will also find out comprehensive spreads that offer you different bet sizes and trade options to work with. This allows you to fine-tune your strategy to match their offerings.

FOREX.com

This platform was founded more recently than others, in the year 2001. But it has quickly risen up the ranks to become a trusted platform among traders. It is designed to meet the requirements of both new and seasoned traders.

The pricing is transparent, allowing you to choose the option that fits your capital availability. You also get to work with different kinds of accounts and each account gives you a unique benefit. In one account, traders pay the spread for every trade that they make while in another, traders are charged a small commission, but the spreads are smaller.

Each account has its own benefits and spread types. However, one of the things that you should be cautious about when using the platform is that there are high levels of risk involved. Sure, you do get bigger rewards for it, but you have to have a proper strategy in place to work on the platform.

City Index

The platform is regulated according to the rules established by the European Securities and Markets Authority (ESMA). This allows the platform to provide you with features such as leverage limit, where you cannot simply apply for any amount of leverage, and negative protection, where you do not lose more money than you place into the platform. You can also apply for stop-loss protection, but you have to shell out a premium amount for the feature. Ideal for beginners, City Index provides you an opportunity to test out your strategies.

XTB

XTB is almost like a one-stop platform to cater to a wide variety of investment needs. You can enter into markets such as shares, indices, forex, metals, and even cryptocurrencies. It also follows certain regulations as it is registered with the Financial Conduct Authority (FCA). You get to use the xStation 5, the primary interface of the XTB, which is easy to use and provides all the pertinent information through charts, watchlists, menus, and notifications. The layout is friendly for new users and provides enough information to attract seasoned traders.

With your chosen platform ready, let us get down to one of the most important steps in Forex trading: determining your position size.

Determining a Position Size and the Importance of Using a Formula

Most traders are of the opinion that you need to pay attention to your entry and exit as they are the most important factors. That is not entirely true.

Determining your position is more important.

You may have created the best strategy in the world. In fact, you might be a math genius whose mind works like Sherlock Holmes, but if you do not know your position size, then all those math tricks won't help you. That's because if you know your position size, then you will be able to gauge how much risk you are about to take.

We have already seen how you can choose between different options for your position size, which are indicated by lots. You have your standard, mini, and micro lots, each one provided you with specific units of a currency (with standard giving you 100,000 units, mini giving 10,000 units, and micro 1,000 units).

When you are looking at the risk, they are further divided into two forms: account risk and trade risk.

Let us see how all of these factors fit into the entire idea of picking the ideal position.

Step 1: Establish Your Account Risk

Before you can even determine your position size, make sure that you have a clear rule for your account risk. You need to set a percentage of your capital as the risk limit. Professional traders often stick by the 1% rule where they only risk 1% of their account for a trade.

Let us assume that you have around $5,000 in your account. If you use the 1% risk rule, then you are only going to risk about $50 per trade. If you like, you can even go lower and perhaps only choose 0.75% as a risk rule, but as long as you do not exceed 1%, you should be fine.

However, the 1% rule is not one set in stone. You can even choose to have a 3% risk rule or a 5% risk rule. One of the most important things to remember is that you do not change your rules between trades or it might become difficult to keep track of your risks.

Step 2: Find Out Your Pip Risk

Your next step is to focus on the trade itself.

You need to establish your stop-loss point and your entry location. Ideally, your stop-loss point should be close to your entry point. But make sure that you do not place it too close or else your trade might stop even when a small loss occurs. In the long run, a small degree of loss is always part of the trade. Let them happen.

To calculate the pip risk, you simply have to take the difference between the entry point and the stop-loss point.

When you have established the distance between your entry point and the stop-loss point, then you can choose the ideal position size for your trade.

Step 3: Get Ready to Determine Your Position Size

Now you can finally determine your position size. To do so, you have to utilize the below formula:

Pip Risk Value x Pip Value x Number of Lots in Trade = Amount Placed For Risk

Here is all the information that we already know:

- We know the amount placed for risk, because that depends on the risk value we have set for ourselves, whether that is 1% or 3% of the capital (refer to Step 1).

- We also know the Pip Risk Value which we calculated using Step 2.

- Finally, we know the pip value which we can find out by simply referring to the currency pair itself.

When you put in the numbers, you finally get your Lots in Trade, which is your position size.

Time for an example.

Let us take the earlier example where you have $5,000 in your account. You have decided to use a risk percentage of 1%. This means that for each trade, you are going to risk just $50. What can you do with this amount? You can get a mini lot.

Each lot has a fixed amount for pips, or the pip value. You can find this out on your trading platform itself or your broker will be able to supply you with the information.

Now, you decide that you are going to trade with EUR/USD which is selling at 1.1366 (bid price) and buying at 1.1370 (sell price). Let us assume that you have placed your stop-loss point at 1.1360, which means your pip risk is now set at 10 pips (1.1370 - 1.1360).

You now have all the information required to fill in the formula. Simply substitute the numbers and you will be able to find your position size.

Chapter 5 - How to Tackle Trading: So Many Approaches You Can Choose From!

The First Option: Technical Analysis

When you are using technical analysis, you are making use of volume and price data to make a speculation about future movements. The fundamental idea of technical analysis was established by Charles H. Dow, who based his techniques on the behavioral patterns of investors, movement or prices, and on psychology. If you choose the movement of prices as your criteria for making an analysis, then that becomes a technical analysis.

When you look at charts that do not feature anything more than the price movements of a specific currency, you will notice that the market moves during trends. Which means that all the information you require for conducting technical analysis is available within the charts of a currency.

We have already seen how we can gain whether we are in a bull market or a bear market. But in order to make the gain, you need to understand the trend lines and make informed speculations.

Technical analysis makes use of patterns and indicators. Patterns are certain forms that are repeated over time while indicators are mathematical functions that are used on the range of prices available in a chart.

One of the important components of a technical analysis is the support and resistance levels. When levels break downward, then they are referred to as support and when they break upwards, then they are referred to as resistance.

Price Action

Price action occurs because of the flow of orders, which in turn comes from the buyers and sellers in a market. Price action will reveal to you how fast operations are taking place in the market, where trades are buying and selling (and what currency they are focused on), and also any specific bias in the market (if any exist). Price action relies on finding patterns.

Patterns are recognized on charts by drawing geometric shapes around certain areas to indicate a pattern. These shapes are not drawn by the platform. Rather, you might find yourself applying a circle here, a triangle there, or a semicircle on another spot to see if there is any underlying meaning in the chart data.

Pattern recognition is not easy. You have to be used to the platform you are using until you can start recognizing patterns or trends.

Another point to remember is that technical analysis is rather subjective. John and Mary may be looking at the same chart, but that does not mean that

John and Mary will come to the same conclusion. Who are John and Mary? We don't know. Just pretend they are two traders who are not as smart as you (because you have this book after all).

Advance and Retreat

When you are looking at a chart, you will notice two types of moves: impulsive and corrective.

An impulsive move happens when there is a sharp movement in the direction of a particular trend.

On the other hand, a corrective move happens when the movement occurs in the opposite direction.

When there is an impulsive move, then it usually indicates the fact that there has been an influx of large amounts of capital into the market. This causes sellers and buyers to arrive at a particular level and have a specific direction in mind. It could also be caused by a cascade in the price, occurring due to a large number of stop-losses that are still pending. Impulsive moves have the most consistency because the flow of order is tuned towards one direction (and a rather predictable one at that). If you can identify impulsive moves, then you will be able to gain some incredible trading opportunities (translation: money money!).

On the other hand, you have corrective moves. These could happen because of two situations:

- Profits have been taken after the occurrence of an impulsive move.

- A mixed number of buyers and sellers are present at a certain level and that level has the potential to become a reversal point.

When a corrective move occurs, then there are usually not many opportunities to conduct a good trade.

When you understand the duration it takes from one move to another, then you might receive an idea of just how long you might have to wait for the next continuous move.

What are the different trends that you can derive from a technical analysis? Let us focus on some.

Trend Indicators

Moving Averages

Moving Averages is a type of indicator that shows you the average value of a currency pair over a specific period of time. Moving Averages, or MA for short, are best used for identifying momentum and seeking out areas of potential resistance and support. Traders also use MA for checking the direction a particular trend is taking.

When using Moving Averages, you can make use of several variations.

Simple Moving Average (SMA): You calculate this MA by adding the closing price of a particular trade or currency across a number of time periods and then divide that by the number of time periods.

Exponential Moving Average (EMA): There is no significant difference between SMA and EMA, except that EMA gives more weight to the latest data and information.

Limited Weighted Moving Average (LWMA): The LWMA also gives priority to the latest data. However, the way to use it is completely different than EMA. The price of a particular period of time is multiplied by the position that price takes in the series of data. All the results are added and the final number is divided by the number of time periods.

Bollinger Bands

These indicators were developed by John Bollinger and they allow traders to compare the relative price levels and the volatility over a particular time period. The name of the indicator is actually apt: it includes three bands that focus on the price trends of a given currency pair.

Bollinger bands are useful for traders in identifying periods of extremely low and high volatility. They are able to provide insights into the fact that prices can reach such extremes that they cannot be sustained, eventually allowing the trader to decide if he or she would like to cut losses or use another strategy in place.

Commodity Channel Index (CCI)

This indicator was developed by Donald Lambert and plays a particularly important role in determining whether a currency has been oversold or overbought. Traders have also used the CCI to figure out the troughs and peaks in the prices of currencies and to find out what possible changes can occur in the trend line.

The Second Option: Fundamental Analysis

Economic Release

To understand fundamental analysis, it is better to start with an economic release. Basically, this release is an official report released by the central banks to the press. Other parties involved in the creation of this report includes governments, the Federal Reserve, large financial institutions, and analytical and research departments who are responsible for working with economic data. These releases are always made available to the public. And this becomes useful for Forex traders.

When traders work their trade based on the news, they need to have reliable information to make quick judgments. These traders are very attentive to the economic release, absorbing the information like a sponge. Some of the main components of the economic release that concern the traders are gross domestic product (GDP), balance of payments, sentiment and confidence reports, prices, leading indicators, spending figures, employment, housing, and monetary policies.

Entering Fundamental Analysis

We are now ready to explore fundamental analysis more. The reason we talked about the economic release is that one of the main sources of data for fundamental analysis is the information provided by the release. But additionally, fundamental analysis also includes political data as sometimes politics can influence the economic regulations and advancements of a country. In fact, the politics of the country can indicate the confidence various factions have with the government of the country and this, in turn, can reveal the status of factors such as foreign investments.

Fundamental analysis also includes the review of macroeconomic indicators and the stock market as well.

When working with fundamental analysis, the existing inflation rate, foreign currency, and monetary mass all come into play. For this reason, governments have increased the frequency of the releases so that traders are able to compare them easily with previous reports. This makes it easier to generate forecasts about the direction the currency is taking and how it could evolve in the near future.

Traders typically start with the primary analysis of data and several factors are important for this analysis:

Economic growth: Traders usually discover this by using the quarterly published figure of the country's GDP. When traders notice that the GDP of a country is rising, then that typically signifies a shift in the capital. This shift occurs because there has been a rise in the savings and consumption in the country. Traders value the consumption increase and make their trades accordingly, having positive sentiments about the currency. However, an excess of growth is not a good indicator. This is because there are chances that the country could eventually deal with inflation tensions and force the Central Banks to change their interest rates.

Inflation: Typically, when currencies have high-interest rates they are considered favorable because of the fact that they can contain inflation rates and of course, the chance to attain high profits. Which is why, when looking at inflation, traders will also look at the Central Bank's changes.

Unemployment: The rate of unemployment is sometimes difficult to measure accurately, but it is nonetheless a very important component and indicator for traders. The main reason for this is that it determines the consumption and income levels for families. If the unemployment rates rise, then the currency of the country falls so hard that it might just punch a hole through the financial basement. When the unemployment rates drop, it helps elevate the currency's value.

Trade Balance: A currency quote can attain an equilibrium, which happens when there is stability in the balance of payments. If the country has a trade deficit, then it suffers due to a drop in the currency reserves, which eventually causes a drop in the value of the currency as well.

Stock market: Inflation, growth, and even unemployment are just some of the factors that are involved in finding out the value of the currency. Every single day, the evolution of a currency has a big impact on the assets markets, in particular, stocks. When investors have positive sentiments about a country, then they increase investments into that country, which in turn propels the stocks and assets to new heights. With the arrival of different currencies into the market, the value of the currency of the home country will become strong.

The Third Option: Market Analysis

When you are performing market analysis, you are taking into consideration a lot of factors. Let us look at a few of them.

Gross National Product (GNP)

The GNP is an indicator of the performance of the global economy. However, when used on a macroeconomic scale, then it is the total of the investments, consumptions, the net volume of transactions, and government spending. In the U.S., the GNP refers to the total of the goods and services provided by the residents of the country, either within its borders or in international territories. When the GNP increases, it improves the situation of the currency.

Gross Domestic Product (GDP)

The total number of goods and services produced by companies in the United States, whether they are domestic companies or foreign entities is indicated by the GDP. Within the U.S., there is little difference between the GDP and the GNP. However, in countries outside the United States, GDP figures are more popular. For this reason, the U.S. release data in both GNP and GDP. When it comes to the currency, the higher the GDP, the better it is for the currency.

Consumption Spending

While the fact is that the spending habits of consumers are purely psychological, it is still a powerful indicator of the economy. Consumer spending habits indicate the confidence they have with the country. Consumer confidence is also calculated as a method to explain why they have a tendency to replace their saving habits with spending habits. When the consumer's spending index increases, the consumer's confidence increases, and that eventually leads to a rise in the value of the currency.

Investment Spending

The gross domestic spending or investment spending consists of inventories and fixed investments. When investment spending increases, it improves the economy, which eventually causes improvements in the value of the currency.

Government Spending

When the government spends, it spends! The sizeable amount of money that the government works with impacts various other factors. Let us take an example to highlight this point. Before 1990, the military expense of the United States had a significant role in the employment rate of the country. The higher the government spending, the better it is for the currency.

Net Trade

Another important factor of the GNP is the net trade volume. After the rise in globalization in the 90s, the United States received a great boost in its ability to compete abroad. However, GNP did not catch on in other countries of the world. So while it does play an important role in the economy of the United States, for all intents and purposes, the GDP is presented to the world. And an increase in the net trade figure always shows an increase in the value of the currency.

Industrial Production

When countries shift away from agriculture to industry, this factor becomes an important indicator of the economy. Industrialization also allows the country to grow, improving its technology and adding more employment opportunities. For this reason, Forex traders often use this indicator as a signal for commencing trading. The higher the industrial production, the better the economy.

Capacity Utilization

This term refers to the highest output of production that industries and factories are capable of under normal working conditions and operations. Typically, capacity utilization is not an important indicator in the Forex market. It's just that there are certain conditions where it might provide information to traders. For a stable economy, the normal capacity utilization is around 81.5%. If the number exceeds the 81% mark, then it is an indication that the industry is about to reach a boiling point and is close to hitting its maximum capacity.

When capacity is maxed out, then the traders in the markets are looking for signs of inflation. This is why, the higher the capacity utilization of a country is, the higher the value of its currency. However, if it becomes too high, then caution is the name of the game.

Factory Orders

This indicator reveals the total number of orders made by factories for the manufacturing process. Typically, Forex traders do not use this indicator.

However, when there is a sharp rise in factory orders, then it usually means that there is going to be a boost in the production of goods and services in the economy, which is typically a good sign. High factory orders are always good for the economy and therefore, improve the value of the currency.

Construction Data

When it comes to the U.S. GDP, construction data is often included and if you look at history, then you might notice that it was housing that pulled the United States out of the recession that happened after World War II.

Why is construction data important? Well, the main reason is that this data is linked to the interest-rate levels and the income level of the people. In the United States, the data is represented by the number of home units. The higher the home unit figures are (referred to people actually occupying units, else these units simply become houses), the better the indication of the economy.

Producer Price Index (PPI)

When the U.S. compiles data for the PPI, then it includes numbers from various sectors such as agriculture, mining, and manufacturing. This is why, the higher the number of the PPI, the better it is for the currency.

Consumer Price Index (CPI)

This indicator reveals the change in prices of the goods and services produced in an economy. But we are not talking about any goods and services. We are referring to those elements that are considered vital for the basic needs and requirements of the people. This includes food, internet, transportation, and others.

Fourth Option: Intermarket Analysis

In an intermarket analysis, the traders focus on more than just one single asset or market to figure out the strengths and weaknesses of the markets. What this means is that, instead of analyzing markets individually, this form of analysis looks at the correlations between four of the major markets: currencies, commodities, bonds, and stocks. So instead of looking at, say the bonds, we also take a look at the commodities market along with it to find any connecting trends that we can use for our trades. But there is no point in looking at these markets without understanding how they influence the country's market.

How Does Intermarket Analysis Work?

To perform an intermarket analysis, we are going to require a few tools of the trade, which include a convenient charting program along with detailed and widely available data.

When you start correlating, then you can give the whole results certain scores.

When you discover a positive correlation, then your score can go as high as 1.0. On the other hand, a negative correlation can bring down the score to as low as -1.0. If the score hovers around zero, then it means that there aren't a lot of correlations for you to uncover.

The intermarket analysis depends on the forces of inflation and deflation. During a normal inflationary situation, bond and stocks are positively correlated. In other words, they both move in the same direction. What happens when they move in different directions? In that case, they are known to move in inverse directions, where one factor goes up while the other goes down. This is also termed as a deflationary movement. If they have a more positive direction, then you are going to give them a positive score if they have an inverse direction, they receive a negative score. The scoring process is something that is done by traders solely for the purpose of getting a better understanding of the market.

Chapter 6 - Your New Journey's First Steps - How to Start and What to Do

Fundamentals of Trading

Many brokers provide you with numerous options when it comes to trading accounts. In many of these accounts, you might find a demo account which will allow you to familiarize yourself with that broker's particular features and platform presentation. This means that you can use the demo account to get comfortable working with your broker.

The demo account not only allows you to work with your broker's platform, but also exercise your strategies within a safe environment without the worry of losing any of your funds.

When you practice using a demo account, you begin to build up confidence. More confidence means less emotions. Less emotions means you have laser-like focus.

Once you have perfected your strategy using the demo account, then you have to implement it in your actual trade. Too often, you find traders who end up using a completely different strategy once they begin trading with actual money. They end up losing big time, wondering where they went wrong and unwilling to admit that they had simply not followed the rules that they established for themselves.

This is why, when you are practicing in your demo account, you are creating a battle plan for yourself. This plan is what makes you confident about your trades. Do not change track when you get started on the actual platform unless you are absolutely confident that the new direction is where you should be heading.

Another factor to remember is that, while the Forex market is mainly unregulated, individual brokers have to follow a certain set of regulations based on the country that they are operating in. For example, if the broker is located in the United States, then they should be registered with the Commodity Futures Trading Commission (CFTC). By doing so, traders can verify the status of the broker. Some brokers who are not regulated with the aforementioned commission when located in the U.S. do not have any financial regulations. This means that they could stop operations and disappear without a trace with all your money. You, on the other hand, will be left without legal recourse.

Of course, this is not true for all brokers. There are many brokers who have a strong reputation but are not regulated by a particular commission. But ideally, knowing about these regulatory bodies will allow you to choose your broker more effectively. We have already shown you many points you should consider when selecting your broker. This additional step is to ensure that you are trading without any problems.

Before you even think of placing your order, make sure that you have a stable and fast internet connection on all your devices. Sure, your internet connection might be working perfectly on your computer. But what about your smartphone? Does your service provider provide you with stability and speed on your smartphone? If it doesn't, do you think you could choose a better data package or a better service provider?

What about multiple monitors? It definitely sounds cool when others do it.

It is not exactly mandatory, but it might help you when you are multitasking. You could use one monitor just for your trading platform. The other monitor can be used for other activities such as listening to your music, chatting with other traders, watching videos (whether they are for trading or simply catching up on the latest episode of your favorite TV show), or completing any of your daily tasks. There are many traders who work off their computers from home, whether they are freelancing or have the ability to carry out their work at home. In such cases, they make use of two monitors so that they can perform their daily tasks but also stay tuned to the price fluctuations happening in the market.

Also, make sure that you are in an environment that allows you to trade properly. It might seem convenient when you think about working from home. But if you have family obligations that could interrupt work, then you are better off working from somewhere else that could provide you with privacy. Remember what we discussed earlier: Forex is a business. It cannot be taken as a hobby.

Once you have decided where you would like to trade, then examine yourself. Make note of your habits and your life patterns. These factors help you decide what kind of trader you are. When you understand your daily habits, then you can arrange a strategy accordingly. This will not only help you trade better but will allow you to adjust to your habits. Additionally, we have just shown you a multitude of ways to perform analysis. Don't go into a trade and then figure out what kind of analysis you would like to do. Why not try each of the analysis methods and find out which one fits your trading.

Placing an Order

We are going to start placing your orders. Perhaps you should try today's best, fresh currency with a side order of pips.

Okay, maybe not that kind of order, but on the trading platform, you are going to be dealing with orders a lot, so let's first get down to the fundamentals.

Essentially, you should be aware of the fact that there are different types of orders available for you to place. When choosing your broker, make sure that they are able to provide you with the order that will want to place in the future.

Let's look at these orders and how
they work.

Market Order

This is a common type of order
placed by traders. In a market order, you
buy or sell the currency at the best
available price, but you perform the
buy/sell action immediately. As in, now!

With a market order, you can either
enter a position or exit from an already
held position.

Let us take an example. We welcome
our old friend EUR/USD and here, let
us assume that the currency pair's bid
price is 1.1376 and the ask price is set at
1.1377. This means that if you are going
to buy the currency, it will be 1.1377.

You are going to confirm buy, upon
which your platform or broker will
execute the buy order.

Think of this step as heading over to
an online store and confirming your

purchase. You look at a product and if you are interested, you click buy.

The only difference here is that you are buying currencies instead of a blender (or whatever you use an online store for).

Limit Order

You place a limit order when you would like to enter into a new position or exit the currency position at a particular price. In most cases, you are going to buy below the market or if you are selling, you are going to sell above the market.

Let's take an example. You find out that the EUR/USD is currently trading at 1.1376. You decide that you would like to go short (or in other words, you sell) if the price reaches 1.1396.

Now there are two ways you can do this:

> 1. You can sit in front of your computer or your smartphone (if your trading platform

provides an app) and wait for it to reach the sweet spot.

2. Or you can place a limit order where your platform will execute a sell action at 1.1396 while you go enjoy your yoga class.

There are several reasons why traders would choose to place a limit order.

- You place a limit order if you expect that the price of the currency will reverse after reaching the price that you predicted.

- Limit orders are placed when you have a clear idea of your profits. When you are creating your strategy, you will usually have an idea where you would like to collect profits when a trade is working to your benefit.

Stop Entry Order

You place this order when you would like to sell below the market and make a buy above that market.

Let us assume that the GBP/USD is currently trading at 1.2741. After conducting your research, you have the belief that the price will continue to rise up until it reaches 1.2751, which is the point at which you would like to place your stop entry order.

As with the limit order, you can choose to do one of two things

- Sit in front of your computer to execute the buy order

- Stop entry order + yoga class

Stop Loss Order

As we saw earlier, you place a stop loss order to prevent you from experiencing heavy losses on a trade if the price does not go in the direction you wanted it to.

If the position you are in is long, then you execute a sell order.

If the position is short, then the order is buy.

Let us say that you went long with the USD/CAD at 1.32185. While planning out your strategy, you decide to place a limit on the maximum loss you can bear by placing a stop-loss order at 1.32150.

This means that if the market goes against you, then your trading platform will automatically make a sell order to minimize your losses.

Trailing Stop

This is a type of stop-loss order that moves as the price fluctuates.

Let us take the above example of USD/CAD. You have decided to place a trailing stop-loss order of 20 pips. This means that at 1.32185, your stop-loss is placed at 1.32165. If the price increases to 1.32195, then the stop-loss moves up to 1.32175.

By using this method, you are ensuring that you can keep up with the rising trend but will be prepared if something out of the ordinary happens and the market decides to go against you.

Now that we have understood the various kinds of orders you can place in your trading platform, it is time to move on to the next step.

The Long and Short of It

We already know that when you go long, it means that you are going to make a buy order. When you go short, you are about to execute a sell order. But is that all there is to it?

Let us dive further so you are clear on both concepts.

When a particular currency pair is long, then you are purchasing the base currency and then selling the quote currency. If you go long on it, then you are making a speculation in which you hope that the price of the currency will rise in the future. The position of long is always indicated by the base currency.

On the other hand, when a currency is going short, then it means that the base currency is being sold and the quote currency is being bought. When you go short on a currency, then you are hoping that there is going to be a drop in the market price of that currency. The position of short is usually denoted by the base currency, but that does not have to be the case. Traders look at both base and quote currency when they are going short.

Exiting a Position

One of the things that traders focus on intently is fine-tuning their strategies and making sure that they have opened their position in the best way possible.

However, they forget one vital component in all of this, how to exit. They simply destroy everything they have built with a poor exit strategy.

Here is how to look at it. Imagine that you have boarded an airplane that is going to take you to a far-off location. It is your holiday, after all, and you have decided on heading over to Thailand/Bali/India or if you are located on the eastern side, then you have chosen New York/London/Vancouver (if you are in the middle, well, pick any direction).

As you get comfortable in your seat and buckle up for the ride, the pilot suddenly pops up near your seat. He looks at you gravely and poses this rather strange question:

"Tell me Sir/Ma'am, do you think the take-off is important or the landing is important? I will adjust my flight preferences accordingly."

Flabbergasted, you take a moment to wonder if the pilot is playing a prank on you. His serious expression reveals that this is no joke. He really wants you to answer the question.

"Both," you respond, hoping that he can see the confusion on your face and the intention in your voice, "I prefer you take-off and land perfectly."

Smiling, the pilot nods and heads back to the cockpit while you sit in your seat wondering whether, if you hadn't answered the question, you would have doomed your life and those of your fellow passengers completely.

Think of trading as the airplane. You are the pilot. What do you think you should be doing when you are focused on your strategy? Do you think entering the position is more important than the exit or the other way around?

If you answered both, then you are keeping your passengers safe. By safe, we mean profitable.

And who are the metaphorical passengers in this rather colorful analogy? Why, the currencies of course!

Calculating Profit and Loss

Of course, the whole point of being on a plane is to reach your destination and enjoy the local beer!

In the case of Forex, the local beer is profits. What is a loss, you ask? We should give an analogy for loss as well. If that is the case, then think of loss as an unsavory dish that is about to go MMA on your digestive system.

When you have closed your trade, you take the price when you are selling the base currency and subtract it from the price of the base currency when you were buying it. You then multiply the result with the transaction size to finally show you whether you made a profit or a loss.

Let us look at an example.

Let assume that you have bought the Euro (part of the EUR/USD currency pair) at a price of $1.1278 and then you sold the currency at a value of $1.1288. Your transaction size is basically the lot size. For this example, you have bought the standard lot of 100,000 units.

So let us follow the steps in the formula to find out our profit or loss.

Step 1: Selling price - Buying price

$1.1288 - $1.1278 = $0.0010

Step 2: Take the result from above and multiply it by your transaction size. In this case, 100,000

$0.0010 x 10,000 = $10

Form the above example, we have noticed that you have made a profit of $10. Way to go trader!

Let's try a different approach to the above example. Let us assume that you are working with pounds (GBP/USD) and you have bought the currency at $1.7374 and sold it for $1.7379.

If you apply Step 1, then you will get a result of $0.0005. When you apply Step 2, then you will get $5 as a result.

You just made a profit of $5.

Of course, if your selling price was lower than your buying price, then you will find that your result is a negative number, indicating a loss in the transaction.

With just a simple formula, you can calculate your profit and loss. Here is a recommendation. Make sure that you are keeping a journal where you note down your strategy and the amount of profit or loss that you have made using that particular strategy.

This way, you can change your strategy and then check to see if your profits have improved or your losses have worsened. This method is effective to plan ahead and figure out the best tactics for your trade. Remember this: trading is a learning process and you will constantly be learning something. It is better to have a record of your transactions, strategies, and ideas so that you can apply what you learned.

Account Balance, Leverage, and Margin

Account Balance

We have already had a glimpse into what leverage and margin indicate. But here, we are going to take a step further and look at each of these terms in detail, while also understanding what your account balance means.

The first thing that you are going to do before you even start the trading process is open an account. You are going to go through the process of evaluating these brokers in such detail that even James Bond would be proud of you.

Once you have finalized your option, you are going to go ahead and open your account with the broker of your choice. Some brokers have an approval phase where they evaluate your profile and then decide if you can use their platform.

When your account is approved, you can begin to transfer funds to your account.

One recommendation at this point is to make sure that you are solely transferring the risk money you have calculated (which is 1% of your capital). Sure, having enough money for emergencies might sound like a sound plan, but having enough money to fuel your temptation is not a good way to start off your trading journey. Once you have mastered the platform and your strategies, feel free to transfer as much as you like.

Let's say that you deposit about $500 into your account, then that will be your account balance.

When you have entered into a new position, there will be no effect on your account balance until the position is closed.

Now, your account balance becomes important when you perform a rollover. Basically, when you are performing a rollover, then you are keeping your account open overnight. There is a difference between closing positions after a few hours and closing them by carrying your position to the next day.

Traders manually make sure that they are carrying their position overnight by closing their positions at the end of the day. At the same time, they will open another position for the next day. This new position that they open will be similar to the position that they closed. In other words, it might look like the same position is getting carried over to another day. This process of closing and opening positions can also be done automatically by giving specific instructions to your broker (also it depends on the fact that your broker has this feature available with them).

When they perform a rollover, then a certain calculation is performed, after which the traders have to pay or receive a certain fee known as a swap fee.

If traders pay a swap fee, then their account balance will reduce.

If traders receive a swap fee, then their balance will increase.

Regardless of the situation, both scenarios will affect your account balance. You won't have to worry about rollovers as they are meant for very experienced traders. However, as we were covering the subject of account balance, it was important to bring your attention to it.

Leverage

Leverage is used to give you a bit of a boost in your trading. If a trader intends to take advantage of leverage, then they have to first open a margin account on their platform. Typically, there is a certain amount of leverage provided that is fairly common among all brokers. You get leverage options of 50:1, 100:1 or 200:1. Which of the leverage options you can take advantage of depends on the broker and also the size of your investment. Some brokers do not allow you to take big leverage in order to protect you from incurring hefty losses. Other brokers are more lenient in that department.

But what do those ratios mean?

Essentially, it is the ability for you to control a large amount of money without actually using much of your own money.

Let us see this with an example.

Let's say that you have opened a position and are now in control of 100,000 units (or $100,000). You have chosen the 100:1 leverage option. Your broker will set aside $1,000 for you (this does not have to be the case as you could even choose $2,000 or $5,000, but we will stick with $1,000 for the sake of this example).

Technically, you are now managing $100,000 with a leverage of $1,000.

Let us say that your investment paid off. The value rose to $101,000. This is an increase of $1,000.

If you had invested in the $100,000 all by yourself, then return is $1,000. This is a 1:1 leverage.

But if you made use of a leverage of 100:1 and your broker set aside $1,000 the outcome is a bit different.

When the value increases to $101,000, then you do not just get the initial $1,000, but by banking on the 100:1 leverage, you get 100% of the profit as a bonus. That means you get $2,000 as your total return.

Sounds cool eh?!

But wait. You might have heard rumors of the fact that leverage can affect you both ways. It could harm you considerably. Are these rumors true?

Think of it this way, if you have made a gain, then you have earned $2,000. If you took a loss, then you would lose $2,000 as well.

The above example showed what happens if your loss was around $1,000. But what happens if you lost more, say $5,000? Then according to your leverage, you have lost a total of $10,000!

See where this situation becomes tricky? Think of it this way: whatever amount you gain, you are going to get an additional 100% of it extra. But whatever amount you lose, you still have to shell out an extra 100% of it as well.

It is no wonder that traders are extremely careful when they are working with leverages. In fact, experienced traders never take a leverage unless they have a bank account that would make Bill Gates blush.

Margins

Now we come to the point of margins.

Let us stick to the above example. Now that you are managing 100,000 units of currency, your broker has told you that in order to have a leverage of say 100:1, they would require a margin of 1%. In this example, that would come up to $1,000.

Basically, that $1,000 that you shell out to your broker is a margin. Think of it as a deposit that you place with your broker. If you are successful in your trade, then you receive the margin back along with the profit you have made with your leverage. On the other hand, well, you already know what happens in this case.

Chapter 7 - Your Plan of Action: Crafting Your Battle Plan

How to Build Your Trading Plan

What exactly constitutes a trading plan? Essentially, you are looking at a set of rules that you are going to place before you venture forth and begin trading in the market. These rules should cover every facet of your trading and you should make them as detailed as possible.

However, here is something that you should understand. Just because you build your trading plan, it does not mean that you are going to succeed. It is not your ticket to profits. Nothing can guarantee profits in the Forex market. However, what your trading will do is help you avoid too many mistakes, prevent things shifting from bad to worse, and provide you solutions for various problems you might encounter.

You can never control the market. But you can make sure that you are in control of yourself. A trading plan is essentially a level of control that you place over yourself to ensure that you make trades based on information, keep your emotions in check, and always look for the next course of action.

A trading plan also breaks down your process into simplified chunks of actions. This allows you to work with each action with care and awareness. If an unexpected situation occurs, then you will know where the problem occurred.

Battle Stations! Building the Battle Plan

Your trading plan should fit you. So you should make sure that it fits your skills, personality, and the number of resources available to you. When you are creating your plan, it is imperative that you are honest in your evaluations. If you have a small amount of capital, you should make sure you understand it as a "small capital" and not "acceptable capital". Also, make notes about your emotional responses. Are you prone to anger easily? Do you get depressed when things go wrong?

Yes, everything is important in your trading plan. No detail is insignificant.

Parts of a Trading Plan

Your trading plan should be able to answer the below queries with clarity:

Markets

What are you aiming to sell or buy?

Position sizing

In what quantities would you like to make your purchase or sale?

Risk management

If things go wrong, how much are you willing to lose without having any impact on your life?

Entries

When do you plan to purchase or sell currencies? Include factors such as your availability, the market hours, when you can sit down and read news releases, etc.

Stops

If you are in a losing position, when do you aim to exit?

Exits

If you are in a winning position, when do you aim to exit?

Strategy

How would you like to deal with currencies?

Time frames

How much do you think you can win from a particular trade? (Make sure you place a proper evaluation.)

Now that we have gone through the basics, we are going to focus our attention on the details.

Here is an example of a checklist that you can use (you can modify some of the questions to fit your requirements):

Before entering any position (whether you are going long or short)

What currency pair are you planning to deal with?

Strategy: What are the primary indicators of this currency? What factors influence it? Can you identify any secondary indicators?

Risk areas: What does your chart look like? Are you able to identify the risk areas easily?

Break-even price: At what point would you consider that your trade has made neither a gain nor a loss?

Look into the actual market position and check out the previous activity. Answer the below queries:

Are there any prices in the current trend that are close to the high or low of the previous day?

Were there any prices that indicated a support or a resistance?

What did the economic reports and news talk about when referring to the previous day's trades?

Now, look at your chart in front of you.

Look at the point of entry of your position and speculate on where the trend will be heading.

Situations

You are going long and the trend seems to be going in an upward direction. It has a downward swing that is bigger than two previous downward swings.

You are going short and the trend seems to be going in a downward direction. It has an upward swing that is bigger than two previous upward swings.

You are going long and the secondary trend seems to be going in a downward direction. It eventually swings back up and goes in the same direction as the main trend

You are going short and the secondary trend seems to be going in an upward direction. It eventually swings back down and goes in the same direction as the main trend.

Measure your risk management

Buy Entry Price

Your broker will set up a signal bar. This is an indicator that lets you know whether the price is reaching a high or a low. You can adjust this signal bar to your preference, but it will be available once you open your position. You might notice this as a horizontal line that goes across your chart. You should ideally buy when the prices are above the high of the signal bar.

Sell Entry Price

Look at your signal bar again. You should be selling when the price reaches below the low of the signal bar.

Risk

Have you set a stop-loss? Make sure that you do.

How much risk are you willing to take at this point with the capital that you have?

Are you going for leverage (your answer should be "no" if you are starting out)?

Situation

Never let the positive trade become negative. Establish your stop-loss points so that you can get out of a loss before it gets any worse for you.

Exit Strategy

Take your profits, or if you have still ended up with a loss, go through the checklist and see if there were any errors. Make sure that you modify your strategies where you see fit.

The above example is just one way of preparing your trading plan checklist. Essentially, you are going to have to describe in detail the what, when, and how parts of your trading.

We have mentioned this before but the point becomes more relevant in this stage: make sure that you are maintaining a journal or record of your activities. No detail should be too insignificant. Entry position, stop-loss, date, time, indicators used, leverage taken, and any other factor that was part of your trade should be recorded accurately. When you have filled out the technical data, move on to yourself.

What were you going through when you took the trade? Did you enter a trade in the right frame of mind? Were your surroundings beneficial to you? As you were making your plan, were you interrupted at any point? Did you just wake up from sleep and decide to make a trade because of a sudden surge in excitement?

Each of these factors helps you discover the weakness in your process. You can find out where you went wrong and discover steps to remedy it.

There are many traders who end up giving up after their first trade, frustrated at not knowing where they went wrong. However, with your journal, you know everything there is to know about your trade. Nothing is arbitrary. It wasn't some unknown cause that led to a poor trade.

Here is another checklist that you can prepare to gauge your readiness for the trade:

- Have you tried out the demo account? What strategy have you implemented?

- How many times have you worked with this strategy? Would you like to go and practice some more or are you confident that you can begin your trade with your strategy?

- Were you able to understand the signals and the charts?

- Do you feel confident about your skills and your ability to understand numbers? Can you replicate that confidence in your trade?

- What are your goals? (Don't say "I would like to earn a million dollars" because that is not a goal, it is a target.) You have to think about what you are going to achieve through trading. Are you planning on starting your own business? Are you going to pay for a world tour? Are you buying your house? When you define your goals, you will understand the seriousness of the situation. You will be receptive to lessons and information. You will make sure that you think of Forex trading as a business venture that requires quite a bit of hard work and dedication. More importantly, you will have an idea of when you would like to stop trading.

- Set up separate sections for the money you might make through trading (this is also based on your initial performance).

- Do you think your current technical setup is satisfactory? Do you feel that your router might break down in the near future? Will you need a faster internet connection? If you cannot upgrade your internet connection, how can you make sure that internet speed is not an issue when trading?

- Are you prepared to accept losses? If you are not, then do you require time to get into the right mental frame? This is important because you should not let losses on your trade run for a long time hoping that it might turn around. Sometimes, you just have to accept your losses, get back to the drawing board and adjust your strategy

- Have you met the conditions that dictate whether or not your entry to the trade is ready? Once you meet these conditions, do not second guess your decision. You might not get the same opportunity again. It does not matter if the trade will head in an upward direction or a downward direction. You have made your preparation. Stick to it.

Understanding Risk-reward Ratio

Your risk-reward ratio is a measure of how much you are willing to risk in order to gain a particular reward.

Here is an example: you are about to make a trade and have set your stop-loss at 10 pips. You have also established your take-profit point at 20 pips.

So your risk-reward ratio is now 10:20 or 1:2. This means that you are planning to risk 10 pips in order to get a gain of 20 pips.

The key thing to remember when you are preparing your risk-reward ratio is to identify situations where the rewards are more than the risks. The higher the rewards you can get, the more you are capable of withstanding any future failed trades. What does that mean?

Let us look at the example above. Your risk-reward ratio is 1:2. Essentially, for every $1 that you risk, you are aiming to receive a reward of $2.

Now let us say that in your first trade you made a win. You now have a reward of $2.

You have a positive balance of $2 in your account.

In the next trade, you made a loss. You have now lost $1.

Your balance at this point is $1.

Now, you can go for another failed trade, which will send your account back to zero balance. But you cannot suffer any further losses or you will enter negative balance. (The idea of a negative balance is not referring to the balance of your account. Rather it is just a way to show that you have now incurred a loss on your investment.)

So the bigger the ratio, the more losses you can withstand.

Let's try this with a table.

We have taken a risk-reward ratio of 1:2. You trade might look something like this.

Number of Trades	Loss	Gain
1	$1,000	-
2	-	$2,000

3	$1,000	-
4	-	$2,000
5	$1,000	-
6	-	$2,000
7	$1,000	-
8	-	$2,000
9	$1,000	-
10	-	$2,000
Total	$5,000	$10,000

With the above transactions, you have made a $5,000 profit. Now, if you decided that you were going to risk 6 pips to gain 14 pips, then your risk-reward ratio is going to be 6:14, to 3:7. If you were to replace all the $1,000 in the above table with $3,000 and the $2,000 with $7,000, then you are looking at a total of $15,000 and $35,000. Which means you make a profit of at least $20,000.

The greater the margin on your risk-reward ratio. The greater the profit. However, does that mean that you will always get an equal balance of profit and loss? Let us use the 3:7 ratio and examine the problem in the below table.

Number of Trades	Loss	Gain
1	$3,000	-
2	$3,000	-
3	-	$7,000
4	$3,000	-
5	-	$7,000
6	$3,000	-

7	$3,000	-
8	$3,000	-
9	-	$7,000
10	$3,000	-
Total	$21,000	$21,000

In the above example, you have neither made a loss, nor a profit. That was because your risk-reward ratio was rather high. What if that was not the case? If you were to go back to the risk-reward ratio of 1:2, then you will have to replace the $3,000 with $1,000 and the $7,000 with $2,000. In the end, you get a total loss of $7,000 and a total gain of $6,000.

Which means, you just made a loss of $1,000.

That is essentially how the risk-reward system works. However, when you are actually trading, the situation may not be as clear-cut and simple as the above examples. There are various factors that go into revealing the loss. But to get a general idea, the above examples show you just what could happen when you have a small risk-reward ratio.

Does that mean you have to only trade with a high risk-reward ratio? Not really. Think of it from this perspective. If you suffered only losses, then with the 1:2 ratio, your total loss is $10,000. With the 3:7 ratio, your total loss is $30,000!

The manner in which you choose your risk-reward ratio is based on how prepared you are with your trade, how well you have created your trading plan, and how much capital you have with you. Additionally, some traders have a higher risk than reward. This might boggle some people but it is essentially done by traders when the market is volatile. That way, they give a bigger margin of error in the hopes that the trend bounces back up after a downward direction of the currency.

Combining all of these factors together helps you determine your risk-reward ratio.

Due Diligence – Doing Your Homework

In the current digital age, we are inundated with terms such as "fake news", "scandals", and "conspiracies".

When you look for any news information online, then the most attractive headline catches your attention. Publishers make use of these catchy headlines because they want that reaction from you: to look towards their headline and forget the competition. The news platforms want to make sure you click-through to their articles.

In many cases, the article headline seems to tell a story by itself. The idea of sensationalism means that shocking language is used to blow up a story.

In those circumstances, it becomes your duty to perform thorough research to verify the authenticity of the information you are receiving. If you react to something without due-diligence, then you are going to make some huge mistakes.

For example, one article in *USA Today* mentioned how the Justice Department spent $16 on a muffin during one of their events. The article's title simply read, "How good is a $16 muffin? Find out for yourself"[3].

Your reaction would be, "Wait! They are enjoying $16 muffins when people are starving on the streets? How could they?! #JusticeFromJusticeDepartment."

However, the reality of the situation was much different. In fact, the article was not supported by the real facts. According to Hilton Worldwide, the $16 included the following items:

- Coffee/tea
- Fresh fruit

- Drinks

- Tax

Now that paints an entirely new picture about the Justice Department. Suddenly, you might find your voice changing from #JusticeFromJusticeDepartment to #JusticeFORJusticeDepartment.

That is the case with numerous news articles from around the world. You cannot simply read a small part of the news. You need to make sure that you are performing your own thorough research.

If there was a similar article such as the $16 muffin in an economic situation, then you might assume that a country is spending heavily on something. Time to make a profit! Eventually, you might realize someone had exaggerated the entire story. Now, you have already invested a large amount of capital in the trade and you cannot back down. All you can do is watch your investment disappear into the digital sinkhole of the Forex market. #JusticeForYou

But it is not just the news and economic data that you have to focus on. Make sure that you are going through tutorials and expert feedback with the same due diligence. Research more about your broker to find out any hidden charges or regulations that might come back to haunt you in the future. Make sure that you are truly prepared before you enter a trade.

Setting Entrance and Exit Rules

A lot of traders spend a considerable amount of time trying to discover the best entry strategies. They look for the perfect buying and selling indications and forget about the exit strategy. When you are going to trade, you need to have a balance between the entrance and exit rules.

Let us take a page out of the textbook of hedge fund managers, who focus on both the entrance and exit strategies.

There are four main ways you can enter or exit a particular trade.

Method 1: Single Entry. Single Exit.

In this method, traders place all their bets on a single point of entry. This means they have only one entry position at one price. When they exit, they do so entirely at one price as well.

Method 2: Single Entry. Multiple Exits.

In this strategy, traders make sure that they enter completely using one position, but for their exit strategy, they leave at different points (meaning, each point will have a different price).

Method 3: Multiple Entries. Single Exit.

In this method, traders enter into positions at different prices. However, when they close their position, they do so at a single price (which is typically the total of the various prices they used for entry positions).

Method 4: Multiple Entries. Multiple Exits.

The title says it all. Traders enter into position using different prices. When they exit, they use different prices as well.

Keeping a Trading Journal

One of the things that seasoned traders will tell you is that, more often than not, trading isn't about finding the secret "recipe" to success. It is mainly about having discipline. We have already seen why discipline plays a vital role in your trades. However, one of the ways that you can maintain discipline is by keeping a record journal. Institutional traders, regardless of their rank and their degree of success are trained to keep a journal until the habit of recording their transactions and other behaviors becomes automatic. The main reason for this was to instill a sense of accountability. After all, these traders are dealing with millions of dollars. How did these traders maintain their journal?

One of the habits that they formed was that for every long and short position that they made, for every stop-loss point they set up, every risk-reward ratio that they decided upon, they had to have a solid rationale for doing so.

It was always, "I am doing this because of the following reasons that are based on large amounts of research and information."

They never decided something without a strong foundation to carry their decisions.

Which is why this level of accountability leads to the formation of some of the best traders in the world. You might think that this is an extreme practice and only pertains to traders who are dealing with large sums of money.

On the contrary, it becomes even more important to you.

Why?

Because you are not dealing with someone else's money. You are using your own money.

For banking traders, they receive a fixed paycheck regardless of how poorly they perform. Of course, repeated mistakes mean that they are asked to leave the job. But in essence, they don't have any personal loss. In your case, forget getting a paycheck. If you lose, you are slowly drying up your own reserves. Additionally, institutional traders have multiple chances to make the money back without disrupting their personal lives. If you experience a loss, then you might find your entire life upended.

Now, your journal is different from the checklist and questions that were created when you were building your trading plan.

Here are some of the things you should include in your journal.

Currency Pair Information

In this section, you are going to make notes about the currency pairs and how you have traded with them. This will work best if you have prepared a table and then taken a print out of the sheet.

Here are some of the columns that you have to use in the sheet.

Currency Pair	Current Price	Daily High	Daily Low	10-day High	10-day Low

Target Trades

In this section, you are going to list all the trades that you are going to make. Essentially, you are waiting for the current trade to generate its results so that you can proceed with your next trade.

Let's say that currently, the date is November 1.

Your entry should look something like this:

November 2

- Buy USD/CAD at 1.1712

- Stop loss placed at 1.1700

- Target 1: 1.1760

- On reaching Target 1, Target 2: 1.1790

- No Target 3. High Risk.

With just a few instructions, you have made your next task easier. You have given yourself clear instructions. The next day, let us assume that you had one of those mornings where you just can't seem to find the energy to even move your pinky.

You force yourself out of bed and realize that you need to get back to trading. However, you are in no mood to think straight. What do you do? How can you keep your trades going? Is this the end of the world?

Wait! There is no need to panic. After all, you have already set a plan into motion. Everything will be okay!

Make sure that by the end of the day, you have taken a small portion of your time to create a plan that will help you the next day.

Completed or Existing Trades

Of course, just like you have planned for future trades, you should also be recording your completed or existing trades. Spend some time looking through the trades you have already made to find out any mistakes you may have made. However, not only can you use this section to identify the losses, you might just discover a trend that you wouldn't have otherwise noticed while looking at the charts.

Think of it this way.

When you are talking with your friend, you might inject your responses and questions with a lot of "uhms" and "ahs". However, do you know how many of these blanks are inserted into one sentence? Are you aware of the frequency of these blanks? If you start recording your conversation and then play it back later, you might be surprised by the results.

Reporters and newscasters often record the way they speak and play it back to themselves so that they can improve their speech patterns. They can identify when they are most likely to pause and where they tend to lose track of the conversation.

In a similar way, you are using your journal to track the "uhms" and "ahs" of your trading. You might not be aware that you are making minor mistakes, but when you look through your journal, you might just be surprised by the frequency at which certain actions slip by your awareness.

Why Money Management Matters the Most

You are dealing with money.

Which is why you need to know how to handle money.

One of the key traits that you need to have in order to become a successful Forex trader is the ability to manage your money effectively.

One of the most important rules that you should apply in your life when it comes to Forex trading is to never invest money that you can't afford to lose.

If you cannot afford to invest the required capital into your trading all at one point, then keep a small portion of money that you are comfortable using for Forex trading. Even if you do have the required amount of capital, make sure that you break it into smaller chunks and use one chunk at a time. When you keep small portions, you minimize the risk.

We have already seen how Forex is all about speculation. But it can turn into gambling if you decide to spend money without being cautious about it. You are making informed decisions and one of those decisions is realizing that you cannot spend all your money in one go.

Next, try and open a small account where you are dealing with micro pips. This way, you are not investing large amounts and even if you suffer losses, it might impact you, but not to an extent where you lose big.

In the world of Forex, ensuring that you are keeping a close watch on your money is what separates a successful trader and one who suffers heavy losses.

Chapter 8 - The Best Tools for the Job: What Every Winning Trader Uses

It's All in the Software

When you are working in the Forex market, the right software helps you connect to the market, gives you regular updates, and essentially completes all the transactions that you would like to make.

You could say that your software is your portal to the world of Forex trading, and that is putting it mildly.

There are many criteria you can use to select the ideal software for your Forex requirements, but here are some of the essential points.

Regulatory Compliance

Many of the software options that you come across will be regulated by the authority in their home country. This is vital when you would like to have a level of assurance when making trades. When software follows regulations, it established a sense of integrity.

Just because the software has some cool graphics and a colorful interface, it does not mean that you should definitely trust the software. Make sure that you are performing your own background checks and checking trusted reviews.

Commissions

Different software programs have different commissions. So when choosing your software, make sure that the commission structure is right. Additionally, there are many software options that give you access to additional features for a premium amount. If this is not the kind of thing that you are comfortable with, then you are better off trying some other platform.

Software Features

Look at all the features available to you and decide if what you are provided will suffice for the work that you have to do. Sometimes, you might find out that choosing another software or a different version of the same software might give you the features that you are looking for.

Customer Service

At the end of the day, nobody is going to have a perfect experience with a software. But that is something to be expected. Which is why every software provider maintains their own team of customer servicing professionals ready to bail you out of a jam or give the occasional *"did you try turning it off and turning it back on again?"* suggestion.

You might need assistance navigating through the complex mechanisms of the software and you might even need expert help in order to guide you through it. This is why you should make sure you've checked out reviews about the customer service team working for the software.

MetaTrader 4 (MT4) and the bigger, shinier, MetaTrader 5 (MT5)

Time to go Meta!

MetaTrader is essentially a trading platform that provides you with a portal to numerous global trading markets. You might find that it is popularly used for trading online in the Forex market, although it does have a reputation for trading in CFD and futures markets as well.

Presently, you can gain access to the MetaTrader by using two of its products, the MetaTrader 4, also known as the MT4, and the MetaTrader 5, also known as the MT5. Let us look at this platform and find out the difference between the MT4 and MT5.

A Brief History

The first version of the MetaTrader came out in 2002. Suffice it to say, it was not really popular among the masses. Ever since then, the company has focused on making changes. They rolled out the MetaTrader 2 which was also not widely accepted widely. The MT3 had the same poor response that the MT2 had.

It was not until 2005 that the MetaTrader became a renowned brand name in Forex trading with the release of the MT4.

Within two years, its popularity grew to such a tremendous scale that between the years of 2007 to 2010, many brokers began to recommend MT4 as the trading platform to use instead of the platform that they were already providing.

In 2010, the brand launched the latest version of the software, the MT5.

MT4 and MT5: What's the Difference?

One of the major differences between the MT4 and MT5 is the programming language that is used by these platforms. The Mt5 makes use of MQL5. The MT4, on the other hand, uses the previous version of the language, the MQL4. What does this upgrade bring to the table? For one, it introduces a new feature called "black box" programming.

Now there is a lot of technical know-how when it comes to explaining what black box programming can do, but it boils down to one thing: the program is easy to use and provides a better foundation for developers of trading platforms and users.

Additionally, the MT5 is faster, allowing for multiple trades to be carried out easily on its platform.

TradingView - The Best Overall Forex Charts Software

We have been talking about how you should refer to charts when you are conducting your Forex transactions. But that begs the question, is there Forex software that will meet your needs and at the same time provide you with tons of features?

The satisfying answer is that there is!

That software is TradingView.

Let's start with a brief summary of what TradingView is all about.

Check out the Awesome View of TradingView!

No, the above title is not their slogan. Although, if they would like to purchase the tagline…

Ahem, we digress.

So what exactly is the TradingView?

It is convenient charting software that also provides traders with the ability to network on the platform. TradingView is ideal for all kinds of trades, whether they are beginners or veterans. It is meant to provide you with a visual representation your trading (which is what we want after all) and supplements that view with tons of information about the trade.

Here are some of the cool features of the software:

Depending on how you would like to approach your trade, you can create simple charts or complex dynamic and multi-layered charts to track a plethora of markets. Additionally, if you feel like it, you can even create your own charts on the platform.

The software comes with different kinds of alerts that you can modify on the platform. Based on what kind of information you require urgent updates about, you can adjust up to 12 different notification settings.

For those who have honed their skills in charting software, TradingView also provides the feature of "Pine Script". What this script allows you to do is create your indicators and charts.

The platform also gives you access to over 50 exchanges around the world, enough to fulfill all your trading needs.

Finally, to add the cherry on the cake, TradingView provides a lot of educational materials. They have everything from videos to podcasts to articles giving you details on how you can trade and how you can manage finances, to how you should be looking at the various charts. Simply put, you have all the information you need to get started on the platform and become acclimated to the Forex world.

You can sign up for a free account, but it is not necessary to view some of the information on the platform. If you would like to simply make a quick reference, then head over to TradingView and you will spot a ticker on the top of the website giving you updates about the popular currency pairs.

Mobile Charting Platforms

Today's world is all about going mobile. If you have a business, it has become vital to target mobile users. It is for this reason that platforms such as Facebook, Google, YouTube, and Instagram all have special marketing campaigns that target mobile users.

In the same way, there are numerous mobile versions of charting platforms that you can access from anywhere in the world, as long as you are connected to a network.

But out of all the platforms available to you, which ones are actually worth looking into? Here are the ones you should consider if you are going to work on charts.

Netdania

One of the highlights of this app is that it provides you with trading strategies and ideas. The creators of the app have marketed the platform as a "personal trading assistant" and in many ways, it does function that way. For example, the app actually gives you a notification to let you know when the right time to go long or go short is. While doing this, it accumulates real-time news and economic information from around the world. Through social networking features, it shares strategies between various traders. This means that you can use the app to copy someone else's trading techniques if they have been successful.

As the app is connected to a cloud platform, you can easily share your info and details between multiple devices. Meaning that if you lose your mobile device, you can always download the app on another phone and get your data back.

Forex Time FXTM

What does Forex Time FXTM have in its favor that most other platforms do not? It has a degree of trustworthiness. After all, it has been used in nearly 180 countries and regulated in numerous regions as well. The platform is designed to work for both beginners, as the app itself is fairly easy to use, and for professionals, as it gives access to advanced features and educational materials. It also offers speedy functionalities and is able to make trades with just a percentage of a second difference between the time you execute and the time the order has been confirmed.

Trade Interceptor

Trade Interceptor is mainly made for advanced users. Though it does have a friendly interface and numerous educational materials to use, it is targeted to those who have more experience dealing with the Forex market. Its main charm is the fact that it provides access to a myriad of indicators that you can use for your trades. The app is also powered by the cloud network, allowing you to transfer your profile to any device. You can even play around with a trading simulator, designed to try out your strategies before you get down to working on real trades.

TD *Ameritrade*

TD Ameritrade makes a comeback! Earlier, we talked about the desktop version of the app. Here, we are going to focus on the mobile version. Not only is the app one of the most established and trusted platforms in the U.S., but it is also regulated (as we have seen before). The information on the app is presented in a clear manner. TD Ameritrade also focuses on other products such as futures, stocks, and options.

Chapter 9 - Making Your First Trade: Step By Step

The Initial Analysis

We have four different analysis options for you to use. Now the question is, is there a way for you to perform an analysis of the market? Is there a secret technique passed down from one Forex sensei to another, finally available to those worthy of seeking its power? Can you do the "Kamehameha" and get your Forex to give you a lot of profits?

The answer to the last two questions is no.

The answer to the first one is, well of course!

Here is a four-step process to help you apply any of the Forex analysis methods you choose.

Step 1: Understanding What Drives the Market

Your first step should be to familiarize yourself with the reasons why many markets are related to each other and what those relationships mean. For example, how do stocks, currencies, and options contribute to the country's market? What factors do each of them share between themselves that allow them to boost or affect an economy?

When something happens to the market, it is not arbitrary. There is always a reason behind it.

For example, when you notice that the stock market is slowly recovering, don't think of it as a good sign and be done with it. Think of why there is a recovery. Is it because investors are hopeful about an upward trend in the economy? If so, what caused this positive sentiment among them?

Step 2: Keep a Record of Trends

Having historical data not only helps you in the short-term, but also in the long-run.

Let's take an example here. Did you know that in the year 2009, Gold prices had risen to a record high? They had practically shot up by 300%.

In fact, one cannot call that a rise. It's like the difference between choosing to climb the stairs to the top and choosing to take the elevator. The Gold prices took the elevator. And that elevator had rocket boosters on the bottom of it.

Now when you look at that information, your immediate thought might be, "wow! I wish I was Scrooge McDuck and I had all his gold. I would have sold them all!"

But then there are those who are skeptical about the rise. Most people consider these skeptics as party poopers, but they have a point. Ask yourself this, why did the Gold prices rise anyway?

Here is a free life lesson for you: if something is too good to be true, then it usually is.

When The Guardian covered this story, they had a very interesting angle[4]. While there could have been many reasons for the sudden rise in Gold prices, one of the most debated ones was the fact that the U.S. dollar had lost status.

Now imagine if the situation were to happen again. What would you do? What would your reaction be?

Step 3: Look for Trends in Other Markets

If you are trading the USD/JPY, then you should not just be focused on the U.S. market. You should look at what is happening in the Japanese market. Check out factors such as their exports, whether the Bank of Japan is planning to intervene in the Forex market, if trade relations between the U.S. and Japan are steady (in fact, check if their relationship has turned sour in any area) or if there has been a new fiscal policy in Japan. Any information that you can gather is beneficial to you.

Step 4: Timing is Everything

Know that you don't have to only use analysis to look at trends or information.

You can actually find out when to trade.

If you are still skeptical about making a move, then perhaps the best way to enter into the trade is to let the analysis give you a story.

Starting the Platform

You are now ready to enter the Matrix.

Think of yourself as Neo about to kick some Forex posterior. Be confident. Be analytical. Leave your emotions at the door.

Before you boot up the platform, make sure you are following the steps mentioned in this book. Keep your journal near you. Start up any charting platform that you may need.

Once you are ready, think of the opening position. Know that from this point onwards, you are going to be making calculated decisions. So be prepared for it.

Opening the Chart

At this point, we could let you know that having two monitors might be useful for you. But it is not vital. There are many traders who only need their trusty MacBook to work with their trades.

You might have already booted up your chart. But make sure that everything is running smoothly. Keeping both the trading platform and the chart open, switch between the two and see if there is any lag in the computing speed. When you are in the moment, looking at prices and making calculations, you are going to be switching between the two software a lot. So make sure everything is running smoothly.

Adding Indicators

If you are using the MT4 or MT5, then you can download custom indicators directly from their website.

- Once you have downloaded them, head over to the install directory in your computer and open the "Data" folder.

- In the Data folder, open the folder named MT4 or MT5. Then open the Indicators file.

- Now open the files that you have downloaded from the website and copy them.

- Paste them into the Indicators file.

You are done.

How do you use these indicators?

- Boot up the MT4 or MT5.

- On the top, choose the "View" option and then head down to the "Navigator" option. Click on it. A window will pop up. Navigate to the Custom Indicators folder. You should be able to see your newly installed Indicator.

- Simply double click it to activate it.

Placing the Order

When you are ready to place orders, simply head over to the "New Order" button. You should be able to spot it in the standard toolbar that comes with the software.

- You will typically be shown a new window. In this window,

you are able to select the
currency pair that you would
like to trade in. Go ahead and
make your selection.

- You might notice an "Order
Type" option in the same
window. Click on it and then
select the "Market Execution"
option.

- Time to enter your position
size. Remember your lesson
on lot sizes. This is where it
comes in handy. For example,
you know that one standard
lot is equal to 100,000 units.
What should you do if would
like to purchase only 2,000
units of a standard lot? You
simply enter 0.02 in the
volume field.

- You also get the opportunity
to add any comments about
your trade in the space
provided. Here, you can make
any important notes that you

think you might need to refer to in the future.

- Finally, you have to choose whether you would like to execute a Sell order or a Buy order. Make your selection and click Accept. A new dialog box will pop-up to confirm your order.

Wait a minute! What about stop-loss and take-profit options? Hit the panic button!

Calm down Grasshopper. We got you covered.

If you would like to add a stop-loss command or a take-profit command, then you have to edit your existing trade. To do so, head over to the tab that says "Trade".

- Here, you will be able to see all your trades. Find the trade that you would like to modify.

- Right click on your trade and then select the option

"Modify or Delete".

- Next, you simply have to navigate to the stop-loss or take-profit field and then enter the value you would like to establish.

- Simply click on the "Modify" button and you are done!

Order Confirmation

Now you might be thinking to yourself, "Why couldn't I just add the stop-loss and take-profit order while I was creating the order?"

The main reason is that when you create your first trade, you will notice that these options are actually disabled by the system. The reason? To make sure that you get to jump into the trade as soon as possible.

Should you like, you can always enter the stop-loss or take-profit values by enabling the options in the beginning. But it is better to get your trade going and then add the changes later.

The Waiting Period

Remember how we talked about the fact that the Forex market is a three-step market? This is why you won't have to wait for too long before your order is confirmed. Typically, it is a matter of minutes, depending on the currency that you have chosen, the values you have entered, and the other options you have enabled.

Trade Complete

Once everything checks out, you will receive a notification letting you know that the trade has been completed. From this point onwards, you are going to use all the tricks that you have learned so far to make sure that you are going to get the most out of your trade. Do not go with the expectation that you are going to get a successful trade on your first try. Have a mindset in which you are aware that your trade could go both ways.

When you have the right mindset, you won't be emotionally distraught or disappointed.

Chapter 10 - The Scalping Strategy: What Winning Traders Do to Profit Quickly

Why scalping and how does FOREX scalping work?

In the world of Forex, scalping is a method of trading where you engage in taking small amounts of profits on a regular basis. How do you accomplish this?

You go long and short several times a day, only choosing to take in small amounts of profit but aiming to rack them up so that, by the end of the day, you have a large enough total profit in your hands.

When you scalp in the Forex market, then you are using real-time analysis to work on the currencies. The reason you use this type of analysis is that you are going to hold the position for a really short time and then close it with the aim of making a quick, but small, profit.

You essentially work during those times of the day when there is a large amount of traffic and quickly buy a small number of pips.

What you should remember about this method is that you have to be in front of your computer the whole time. You are not going to be playing the long game here. You need to make sure that you are not going to get distracted while you are engaged in scalping.

Forex Scalping Strategies VS Other Trading Strategies

People who engage in scalping are specifically called scalpers while those traders who use any other form of strategy are collectively labeled "day traders". So why is there a distinction between these two forms of trading, as though scalping is a unique strategy on its own?

Let us examine this.

The best way to understand the differences is by categorizing them based on certain factors. We'll start with the time.

Timeframes Used by the Two Forms of Trading Strategies

There is a major difference in the timeframe adopted by scalping in comparison to other strategies. What exactly is the time used by the scalping and the others? Well, when a trader engages in scalping, then he or she opens a trade and closes it in a matter of minutes. Most traders aim to complete the trade within 1 or 2 minutes while some others (especially those who are getting started on the platform), take about 4 to 5 minutes to complete the trade.

Regarding The Others (we are going to use this term to describe every other strategy that is not scalping), the trade takes place over the course of 1 to 2 hours (or more).

Some traders use both strategies. They open up a trade using The Others and while that is open, they engage in some scalping. However, doing that is a big risk as it involves more capital, the capital being split into different directions, and the requirement of extra attention. In fact, if you are not used to it, you are going to be overwhelmed really quickly.

Account Sizes

Scalping involves high risk. Because you are trading within such a short timeframe, you are not giving the trade a lot of time to go in a particular direction. This is why scalpers have a large account size.

On the other hand, The Others are used by traders who have a fairly average account size. This is because traders can work with small amounts and then keep their trade active for a fair amount of time.

Difference in Experience

Scalpers are highly focused on their trade. They are well-versed in the knowledge of the market. This is because they are not waiting for a result. They have a strategy and they are in and out of the trade quickly. This is why scalping is a strategy based on skill and a fair bit of experience on the trading platform.

Quick Results

As scalping involves quick trades, it also yields quick results. It could be a profit or a loss and once the scalper recognizes the result, he or she has already moved on to the next trade.

Most scalpers keep a particular target for a day. This could be the number of trades carried out or a certain amount of profit earned (which typically falls into a particular range).

If trading in The Others is like watching Dwayne "The Rock" Johnson fight, full of big impacts and methodical movements, using scalping is like watching Bruce Lee, in and out before you know it.

What makes for a good FOREX scalping system?

In order to have a proper scalping strategy, there are a few points that you need to take into consideration. Let us look at some of these points.

Liquid Pairs

Some of the most liquid pairs are listed below:

- EUR/USD

- USD/CHF

- USD/JPY

- GBP/USD

Why is it important to focus on liquid currencies? This is because these pairs have a tight spread or in other words, they usually have high trading volumes (ideal for scalpers).

Getting Busy

You need to make sure that you are trading at the busiest times of the day or else you are not going to get a lot of action. And you need a lot of action! Here are some of the busiest times of the day:

- 2:00 am - 4:00 am EST

- 8:00 am - 12:00 pm EST

Therefore, your best bet is to make as many trades as possible during the first time frame and then wait till the second time frame to continue with your trades.

Spread

Spread will play an important role in your overall returns. This is why you will need to pay close attention to your spreads.

Test the Waters

Try working with one pair first before moving on to the others. Many traders end up trading with two or more currency pairs and the tactic backfires on them. Furthermore, if you put all your energy into one pair, then you have a better chance of getting a successful trade.

No Need for the News

Do not pay too much attention to any big news announcement. They can confuse you about your trade and you might make a move out of sheer panic. And that is not something we want. After all, we are doing everything possible to control our emotions. However, the news does play an important role in future trades (either in the next time frame or the next day).

The Simple Scalping Strategy - Scalping At Resistance and Support Levels

This is a really simple method to scalp. What you do is that you buy the lows and then fade the highs.

For this scalping strategy, you need to be aware of two very vital points:

- Trading range

- Low volatility

The trading range allows you to select where you would like to place your longs, shorts, and stops. On the other hand, the low volatility helps you avoid the risk of a market or trade going against you sharply.

This method is not only used by seasoned scalpers, but it is perfect for beginners who are getting introduced to the platform.

1-Minute Scalping Strategy

In this strategy, you make use of a special indicator that comes with the MT4 known as the predictive EMA. Typically, this indicator is already available with the system when you get the MT4. This strategy makes use of the typical MA indicator but is slightly modified so that it works on charts that are based on 1-minute durations.

The first thing you are going to do is set up the EMA. To do that, make sure that your MT4 or MT5 is open in front of you. Head over to the Insert option, then work your way over to the Indicators section. Move to the option titled Trend and click on Moving Average.

In the dialog box that pops open, you will see two options: Period and Shift.

Enter the following values:

- Period - 25

- Shift - 8

Then continue clicking OK until the EMA has been set up.

Next, you have to set up two more EMAs. Follow the same steps as above but for the second EMA, the values are:

- Period - 50

- Shift - 15

For the third EMA, the values are

- Period - 100

- Shift - 30

Once the EMA has been set-up follow the below strategies.

Long

- Go Long when the 25 EMA first crosses the 50 EMA. Eventually, both the 25 and 50 have to cross the 100 EMA.

- Buy on the "candle" indicator (this is the shape of the various bars in the indicator, they look like candles).

- Your target should be from 5 to 10 pips and you should have placed a stop-loss order of anywhere from 9 to 12 pips.

Short

- Go Short when the 25 EMA first crosses below the 50 EMA. Eventually, both the 25 and 50 have to cross below the 100 EMA.

- Sell on the "candle" indicator.

- Your target at this point should be the same as for the Long strategy, from 5 to 10 pips with anywhere from 9 to 12 pips for a stop-loss order.

Conclusion

What you have seen is just the beginning.

But the beginning is essential to lay down the foundation for future successes. Too often, traders fail in the basics and then continue to struggle when they are trading in the future.

One of the things that you should understand is that Forex is a real market. It is also one of the largest financial markets in the world. Which is why every strategy you implement matters. Every move you make could make or break the trade.

People are often looking for the "treasure chest". The once in a lifetime move that will get them millions of dollars in their bank accounts. Forex does not work that way. In fact, the "treasure chest" you are looking for - the big treasure - is right there within you. It is your brain.

Every lesson you learned here - from understanding the Forex market to getting into the mindset of a winner to knowing about different analysis methods - are there to power up your brain.

And within there lies your biggest treasure: the knowledge that you have which is the rubies, diamonds, and other precious gems of your treasure chest.

All you have to do is know how to transform those rubies and precious gems into dollars.

This book has given you all the resources you need to get you started on your Forex journey. It is your primer into the world. Your handbook to understanding the variety of information you are going to face.

At the end of the day, you are going to take that with you.

Happy trading.

References

Scutt, D. (2016). Here's how much currency is traded every day. Retrieved from https://www.businessinsider.com/heres-how-much-currency-is-traded-every-day-2016-9/?IR=T

Malito, A. (2018). This guy lost $10,000 trying to time this volatile market — using his credit card. Retrieved from https://www.marketwatch.com/story/this-guy-lost-10000-trying-to-time-the-market-volatility-using-his-credit-card-2018-02-06

Douglas, M. (2001). Trading in the Zone. Penguin Group US.

Lien, K. (2008). Day Trading and Swing Trading the Currency Market: Technical and Fundamental. John Wiley & Sons.

Tharp, V. (2007). Trade your way to financial freedom. New York: McGraw-Hill.

Brown, J. (2019). MT4 high probability forex trading method. CA: San Bernardino.

Notes

[←1]

Scutt, D. (2016). Here's how much currency is traded every day. Retrieved from https://www.businessinsider.com/heres-how-much-currency-is-traded-every-day-2016-9/?IR=T

[←2]

Malito, A. (2018). This guy lost $10,000 trying to time this volatile market — using his credit card. Retrieved from https://www.marketwatch.com/story/this-guy-lost-10000-trying-to-time-the-market-volatility-using-his-credit-card-2018-02-06

[←3]

Hirsch, J. (2011). How good is a $16 muffin? Find out for yourself. Retrieved from https://usatoday30.usatoday.com/money/industries/food/story/2011-09-28/16-dollar-muffin-recipe/50590060/1

[←4]

Rogoff, K. (2010). Why has the price of gold risen 300%? | Kenneth Rogoff. Retrieved from https://www.theguardian.com/commentisfree/2010/oct/03/gold-price-rise-us-dollar-euro

www.ingramcontent.com/pod-product-compliance
Lightning Source LLC
Chambersburg PA
CBHW030502210326
41597CB00013B/763